Curate This!

The Hands-On, How-To Guide to
Content Curation

www.CurateThisBook.com

To Beth!

Go Forth and Curate!

By Steven Rosenbaum

Copyright © Magnify Media, LLC, 2014

About the Author

"Curation comes up when search stops working. Curation solves the problem of filter failure."

Clay Shirky

Steven Rosenbaum is both a creator and a curator. He is widely known as one of the leading thinkers and writers on the topic of curation. He is the curator of the nationally known CameraPlanet Archive, the world's largest archive of 9/11 video, now housed at the National 9/11 Memorial Museum. In 2010, Rosenbaum wrote the groundbreaking book *Curation Nation: How to Win In a World Where Consumers are Creators* for McGraw Hill Business. At a time when the word 'curation' was still mostly used by museum PhDs, Rosenbaum coined a new definition for the phrase and explored the foundation of this new kind of man/machine interface. Now, two years later, curation has gone from a theory to a powerful practice. In *Curate This!*, Rosenbaum turns ideas into action... providing a blueprint for the future and a solution to the overwhelming information overload in which the rush of information and ideas inundates us all. Rosenbaum is the CEO of Waywire Networks and the curator In Chief of Waywire.com, based in New York City.

Early Praise for *Curate This!*

Curation will be one of the drivers in the next chapter of the Internet, as we continue to shift from a world of scarcity to one of abundance. Curate This! is a valuable guide book for publishers, marketers and merchants as they seek to leverage the growing importance of curation.

Steve Case
fmr Chairman & CEO AOL, Chairman and CEO
Revolution LLC

Urgent, erudite and entertaining, this is a book from a pioneer who cares (a lot) about what's going to happen next.
Seth Godin, Author, The Icarus Deception

Rosenbaum, the king and coiner of curation, finally shares the method behind the seeming madness of finding, collecting, and contextualizing the infinity of the net.
Douglas Rushkoff
Author, "Program or Be Programmed"

Back in the day, there were, like, 20 magazines. The biggest was Reader's Digest, which just cherry-picked from the other 19 - because who had the time to sift through everything? Now there are a squidrillion media sources, Glut is the disease, and - paging Dr. Rosenbaum - curation is the cure.
Bob Garfield
Author and Host of NPR's On The Media

We're all dealing with a world that's feeding us Too Much Information. "Curate This!" helps us understand curation, why it's important, and how we can provide clarity for ourselves and others.

- Craig Newmark, Founder, Craigslist

Few people make better sense of the complicated world of content and commerce than Rosenbaum. His utterly current take on curation reminds us that without committed curators like Rosenbaum the web would merely overwhelm most of us.

- Merrill Brown, Director - The School of Communication at Montclair State University, fmr Editor-In-Chief, MSNBC

Even in this age of automation where software is everywhere, Steve understands the importance of context, taste and point of view. Human curation is a must have navigational layer in a sea of infinite ideas. Curate This! is a great resource to understand how it's evolving.

- Jason Hirschhorn, CEO – REDEF, The Interest Remix Company

The world is "simply throbbing with rich treasures," as author Henry Miller once wrote. As the information landscape multiplies, you might as well be contemplating a junk heap. Curate This! gives you the tools to find, amplify and enjoy the treasures again.

- Laurel Touby, Founder, Mediabistro.com

Contents

"Curators are packagers of content—your friends are curating content everyday—175,000 tweets per minute."

Mia Quagliarell, Flipboard

Foreword

We are the Network

I've known Steve Rosenbaum since the mid-2000s. We've worked together and over the years, we've grown to become great friends. Before we met in the real world however, I was also a fan of Steve and his work at on MTV News: Unfiltered in the mid-1990s. Little did I know that this person whose work on a show that had a profound impact on me would become someone whom I would continue to admire and respect as his work continued to challenge convention and pioneer new fronts.

MTV News: Unfiltered wasn't an ordinary news program. It was crowd-sourced, where everyday kids and young adults would curate the news based on what was important to them. It was my first real foray into the world of user-generated content. As producer and creator of the show, Steve was essentially a master curator of content and exceptional programming. Arming the MTV generation with cameras and a voice, we were introduced into world that didn't receive popular airplay as told by people who would have their 15 minutes of fame. All of this was well before YouTube and all of the social media we take for granted today.

Steve figured out that if you open the doors to people and what's interesting to them without influence of what mainstream media fed us, he could not only inform us in new ways but also build vibrant communities around people and curated, interest-driven content. This premise would influence my work in media and research.

Steve's vision and subsequent work with Magnify.net and Waywire would also shape a new wave of technology startups, platforms and media channels that would empower everyday experts to create and curate content for networked audiences around the world. More so, content too would evolve in ways where viewing or consumption was no longer enough. Networked audiences too would become part of the story in how they shared, remixed or reacted to the content of others. Impressions used to be a big deal, but it's no longer enough. That's for yesterday's programming. Now it's all about impressions that transform into expressions and how and what people say and share in response to what they find fascinating, though provoking or simply entertaining.

That's the power of the human network and it represents the future of curation, broadcast, connections and media at large.

By the people for the people...

The art of curation combined with social media, its partner in enablement, allows for content to travel to and also through people bringing to life a human broadcast network. This vibrant and highly efficient distribution channel is powering a new era of consumption, dissemination and engagement around relevant information and the communities that form as a result.

In our own way, we are each now programmers of our own digital channels now. Our audiences are the people to whom we're connected and those who are connected to us. Our communities are defined by what we share and what they share and how we interact respectively. We are what we see and hear. We are what we say and don't say. We are watch we share. We are the network.

That's pretty amazing when you stop and think about it.

Brian Solis, author, digital analyst, human

Preface: How We Got Here

"Curation is more than packaging—it is to help readers (discern) what is important in the world."

Maria Popova, Brainpicker

Let's face it - we broke the web.

No one person or company is to blame: we all played our parts. We tweeted, Facebooked, blogged, Flickred, and YouTubed the rolling green fields of a content utopia into a chaotic cacophony of bits and bytes. Our hard drives runneth over, our email is overflowing and it's having an impact on our work, our lives and even our health.

Having overgrazed the commons, we're now headed to the sky; to the cloud, where all information will fit, and where everything will be available all of the time. At first glance, it seems like a new content utopia.

Today, all the talk about content moving to the cloud is warm and fuzzy. The idea that all of the information you might ever want, all of the music you might ever want to listen to, all of the photographs you'd ever take, would all be just a link away seems delightful. However, clouds have a different metaphorical meaning as well and I see storm clouds on the horizon, dark and foreboding clouds.

In "Curation Nation", I foretold a future where human filters became critical, but at that time, the concept of the 'cloud' hadn't emerged. Now the race is on and the mass adoption of the 'cloud' has dramatically accelerated the pace of the human/robot battle. Digital robots are the algorithms, filters, and automated processes that claim to be able to replace human editorial and curatorial judgment. Privacy, authenticity, and our individual digital identities are at stake. Without clear understanding and controls, our most private and intimate details are naked and exposed in the cloud.

How did this happen, and how did it happen so quickly?

Content in the cloud is a natural evolution from content on our desktops and in our devices, but the content creation explosion that has overfilled our inboxes and overwhelmed our social networks won't be solved by moving the growing mass of data from a private realm to a public one, and it won't be solved by robots.

In fact, there's a solution on the horizon that promises to find meaning in the noise, relevance in the maelstrom of user-generated media. It's called curation, and it's the only hope we have of making sense of the exponential growth in raw unfiltered media.

In the pages that follow we'll answer lots of questions - and raise a few as well.

- What are the 'Rules of the Road' for content curators?
- Where should sites draw the line between aggregation and curation?
- What are the potential liabilities and risks?
- How can you create an editorial road-map to blend curation into content creation workflow?
- How can you create a 'curatorial voice' for your content mix?

Then, we'll journey deep into the heart of the curation jungle and learn how digital media sites like BuzzFeed, Upworthy, Waywire, and more, are embracing a curation model. We'll explore software tools that are turning ordinary mortals into curation superheroes – expanding their reach and giving them the power they need to discover, sort and share content across the web.

In "Curation Nation", I promised a future where the lines between content makers and content consumers would blur.

Today – just three years later, we're living in that wonderful, messy world. In "Curate This!" we'll provide a hands-on, how-to guide to content curation. This is a book that turns theory into practice, and explores how curation is revolutionizing fashion, commerce, education, entrepreneurism, and brand marketing,

The concept of curation has rapidly moved from museums to mainstream media. With the right framework, curation can be a powerful tool to help the editorial web meet new challenges.

It's our last chance to humanize the digital web before it's broken beyond repair.

So get your cape and tights – and prepare to scale tall buildings in a single bound. Curation is a superpower, and you're about to help rescue Gotham from its media maelstrom. (Ok, it's a metaphor, but it's a fun one you've got to admit).

How to Use This Book

"People are just more interesting than algorithms."

Noah Brier, Percolate (re: aggregation vs. curation)

Curation is a big word and it means different things to different readers. So, I've broken my mission into three parts. First, in broad strokes, what is curation? What are the rules of the road? What's the best way to understand the mix of gathering, organizing and creating? Of course, your mileage may vary in this regard. An ecommerce site may find that gathering photos and videos about how customers use their products is the right mix for them (0% created, 100% curated), while a publisher with a known brand for the high quality Editorial may want to flip that ratio on its head (i.e., 80% created, 20% curated).

Then, after we've defined what curation is – and isn't - we'll take the cooks tour of some of the curation rock stars helping to shape the space. This isn't a top-ten list and don't be worried if your favorite curator isn't mentioned. It's simply meant to help round out the description of the best practices with some real world efforts and results.

Finally, we'll dig in to actual best practices, tools and, of course, the word that keeps the lights lit, monetization. I hope you find this section of the book the most useful over time and that you use it as a reference tool that you can return to again and again as you test new tools and roll our your curation game plan.

So, feel free to read fast, skim, bookmark and skip. Not every chapter in this book is for every reader and not every tool or solution will solve your problems. Please remember that the world of curation is a fast moving, evolving space, so expect that some of the tools I write about will, over time, emerge as leaders, while others will merge or close down. That's the nature of writing in a space where daily changes in devices, file formats and user behaviors mean that we are still under construction.

Part 1:

Why Curation is Cool, Now.

Chapter 1: Humans vs. Robots.

In November 2012, in a room full of media heavyweights, CEOs and high-tech entrepreneurs, the debate was hardly philosophical. "Will robots overtake humans?" and, in some cases, should they?[1]

The Monaco Media Forum was the site of the showdown and the panel was an esteemed group of thinkers and digital leaders. Bonin Bough, the VP of Global Media and Consumer Engagement for Mondelz International, moderated the conversation. The panel consisted of Adam Singolda, the founder & CEO of Taboola, a leading algorithmic video recommendation technology; Patrice Slupowski, the VP of Digital Innovation and Communities for NExT.com; Orange, the French-based telco; and myself, a passionate advocate for human curation – both as the author of *Curation Nation* and the CEO of Waywire Networks and Chief curator of Waywire.com.

The author, with Bonin Bough, Adam Singolda and Patrice Slupowski

We all agreed that there are jobs that are dangerous or repetitive and these jobs are ideal to be fulfilled by robots. For example, the ATM – I think of them as bank teller robots and I love having those robots at every corner bodega. The ticket machine at the train station or the movie theatre is another great example. These robots add value. However, when I think about the 'tweet bot' - a robot that responds to me when I follow someone on Twitter – my opinion changes. A tweet bot tends to send me a message that says "Thanks for following me," but provides no indication as to whether the message came from a human or robotics that mimic, or even impersonate, a human.

Bough jumped in and shared a story about the moral dilemma of when we should draw the line. He pointed to a site called Weavers that builds automated Twitter characters that take on a life of their own and begin to roam around the Twitterverse. As these Weaver Twitter-bots begin to take on personalities, they take on a larger role in the Twitterverse, overwhelming the humans that power the Web.

Here, I propose a new rule of robotics: that going forward, robots must identify themselves as robots and can't impersonate human beings.

Why would anyone want a robot to replace humans? It may be a right-brain, left-brain conflict. Automation makes things more efficient, more the same, more boring, but humans tend to make things that aren't exactly the same. The nature of human creation is that it isn't algorithmic, but it, in fact, will have connections and relationships that are both logical and illogical.

The danger of allowing robots to do the work of humans is that they are getting close enough to impersonating living people that consumers will start to accept almost 'good enough' content created by robots. For example, take a look at

Jason Hirschhorn's daily newsletter *Media ReDefined*. My theory is that an algorithm could try to replace Jason's formula, but it would miss the 20% of the newsletter where he adds a link to an off-center phenomenon or a music video from the band Joy Division. The human element of *Media ReDefined* is what makes it fun, surprising and engaging. A robot can't do that.

The shift that changes the human-to-robot equation is the sheer volume of content flooding the Web. Digital overload is swamping the current recommendation engines, making the sharp knife of human editorial a better filter than the blunt instrument of algorithmic recommendation.

"Between the dawn of civilization through 2003 **5 exabytes** of information was created.

Now that much information is now created **every 2 days.**"

Eric Schmidt, Google

Case in point: Eric Schmidt, the Chairman of Google said at a conference in 2010, "Between the dawn of civilization through

2003, 5 exabytes of information was created. Now that much information is now created every 2 days."[2]

So, while an algorithm might be able to sort out a collection of quality content, like feature films, music released by a label or books distributed by a publisher, the sheer volume of self-published books or self-recorded music makes the algorithmic approach less and less successful.

The coming shift may not be toward or away from robots. As the believers in the philosophy known as The Singularity suggest, we're approaching a time when robots and humans will find common ground. The year in which this event will happen is 2029, just around the corner. Inventor and futurist Ray Kurzweil says that the day is already foretold. Kurzweil is generally recognized as a public advocate for the futurist and transhumanist movements and sees the merging of humans and technology as inevitable.[3]

For Bough, the question today is: "Where does humanity begin and robotics end? Machine learning and robotics are the same thing. As we move closer to a symbiotic relationship, what are their places in our understanding of humanity?"[4]

For the foreseeable future, the question of where humans and robots share joint custody of the future remains unclear.

However, until then, having robots stop impersonating people seems like a reasonable place to draw the line.

Robots and Editorial – Why Humans Work

The shift from algorithms to human Editorials is perhaps no better seen that with Gabriel Rivera and his two powerhouse sites Techmeme and Mediagazer.[5] The sites, which were launched in 2000, were, for a time, considered to be the poster children for automated content aggregation. Rivera began by using algorithms to grab headlines and deliver topical and timely news feeds. For the first 10 years of the site's existence, it was driven by robots, using 'signals' from online users to move stories up or down on the page. However, as the volume of content choices continued to grow, and audiences became more interested in clarity and how judgments are made about what's important, not just what's popular, Rivera shifted his model and started employing human curators across the globe, from Bulgaria to Australia.

Rivera explains why algorithms will never be able to curate as effectively as humans: "A lot of people who think they can go all the way with the automated approach fail to realize when a news story has become obsolete," said Rivera, explaining that an article can quickly be superseded even if it receives a million links or tweets.

Today, Rivera relies on human curators to manage the headlines that rise up and push down ones that aren't newsworthy. His position today is that any serious tech or political news publisher will always have to provide smart, engaged human curation to break through the noise.

Rivera says that social news isn't a magic bullet either. Your friends on Facebook aren't going to surface what you want as well as a human curator can: "People like to go to the *New York Times* and look at what's on the front page because they have a lot of trust in what [the] Editors decide and they know other people read it."

"We want to do the same thing," he said. "There's value in being divorced from your friends.... I'd rather see what's on the front of the *New York Times*."[6]

Noted Silicon Valley reporter Tom Foremski has been a long observer of the humans vs. algorithm debate.[7] According to Foremski, "I define curation as a person, or a group of people, engaged in choosing and presenting a collection of things related to a specific topic and context. Aggregation employs software (algorithms) and machines (servers) to assemble a collection of things related to a specific topic and context."

Foremski says that aggregation tools can be employed by curators, but the human act of curation adds a layer of value that aggregation alone cannot provide. He points to Techmeme, who he says can produce a "superior, curated product than by machine aggregation alone."[8]

For the longest time, the Silicon Valley venture community was leading the drive to automate and robotize content and examples exist of where robots broke into content creation. Narrative Science, an artificial intelligence company with a product called Quill, used Quill to turn data into 'journalistic' stories that read like a newspaper article.[9] So, who's using robot-written stories? The company says that they have 30 clients using their robo-reporters to turn data into news stories and Forbes now employs them to automatically generate articles about upcoming corporate earnings statements.

As Forbes puts it, "Narrative Science, through its proprietary artificial intelligence platform, transforms data into stories and insights." But Slate, in reporting on the automation of journalism, was pretty bemused. "Don't miss the irony here: Automated platforms are now 'writing' news reports about companies that make their money from automated trading. These reports are eventually fed back into the financial system, helping the algorithms to spot even more lucrative deals. Essentially, this is journalism done by robots and for robots. The only upside here is that humans get to keep all the cash."

Yes, robots are cheaper than humans. Slate makes no bones about that. Reporters are humans and humans can be a pain. "First of all, it's much cheaper than paying full-time journalists who tend to get sick and demand respect." However, the real issue, and opportunity, for a man/machine interface may be the sheer volume of data and content being created, which is sure to increase. According to Slate, "Few journalists have the time to find, process and analyze millions of tweets, but Narrative Science can do so easily and, more importantly, instantaneously."[10]

To be fair, reporting earnings reports, sports scores, even the weather tends to have a pretty formulaic rhythm and style. Therefore, teaching a robot to impersonate a weatherman may not be too tough a trick. However, news, information, analysis and gleaning the importance of these things is very different from gathering what's trending on Twitter and turning it into a 140-character tweet.

Compare Techmeme's human Editorial with the feed on Google News, a fully automated technology. Here's what Google says about Google News at the bottom of each page:

"The selection and placement of stories on this page were determined automatically by a computer program."

Tom Foremski explains the importance of human curation this way: "The human element is important, but it's expensive, which is why Silicon Valley tech companies favor software and machines. Silicon Valley investors fund businesses that are scalable, that can be expanded by simply adding more servers and software." Which is to say that robots are cheaper than humans. However, in a noisy world, humans may add the unique voice and POV that makes your Editorial voice stand out over the competition.

When all of the financial pages are delivering the same robot-created financial text, then which one you read doesn't matter. Foremski nails it with this quote: "People-based businesses are not scalable in the same way (that robots are) - you need to hire more people to do more. People add complexity [and] require management; vacations and labor costs always trend up. In comparison, servers and software costs keep falling and their productivity increases."

Certainly, smart discovery tools that help human Editors see the forest for the trees are ever more important in this massively noisy world. So is actively listening to conversations, posts, tweets and feeds in your area of content expertise, but it doesn't replace humans.

Foremski makes the point with precision: "I see curation as one part of that human essence, a natural human activity that cannot be matched by technology. And curation is where the value lies in improving the organization and usefulness of the Internet." But if you believe that curation requires humans, then what is curation really?

The term "curator" has been around for ages; historically, it had been applied to museums and art galleries. Art or museum curators are heralded as cultural experts who select, organize and present artifacts and works of art for patrons to behold and critique. Digital content curation is similar in that it requires the gathering of information from the Internet, selecting the most important elements, organizing the content and sharing it with others in a concise and easy-to-consume manner.

Marketing expert Rohit Bhargava set out a concise definition of what a curator is when he created his manifesto in 2009.

Manifesto/job description: Content curator

In the near future, experts predict that content on the Web will double every 72 hours. The detached analysis of an algorithm will no longer be enough to find what we are looking for.

To satisfy the people's hunger for great content on any topic imaginable, there will need to be a new category of individual working online. Someone whose job it is not to create more content, but to make sense of all the content that others are creating. To find the best and most relevant content and bring it forward. The people who choose to take on this role will be known as Content curators. The future of the social Web will be driven by these Content curators, who take it upon themselves to collect and share the best content online for others to consume and take on the role of citizen Editors, publishing highly valuable compilations of content created by others.

In time, these curators will bring more utility and order to the social Web. In doing so, they will help to add a voice and POV to organizations and companies that can connect them with customers – creating an entirely new dialogue based on valued content rather than just brand created marketing messages.

– Rohit Bhargava

Bhargava is spot on. Since releasing that technologically profound declaration into the Internet ether, content curation tools, which are tools that allow you to discover Web information specific to your area of interest and then organize and distribute it to your target audience, have taken off. It seems like Internet overload was a problem searching for a solution... and the solution was curation. Ta Da!

Chapter 2: Brands, Native Voice and Curation

In the world of buzzwords, there is no buzz louder than the buzz of "Native advertising," but, as with all things in the evolving world of content and marketing, the buzz sometimes blurs the actual opportunity.

Where is the line between content 'creation' and 'curation'? Can Native curation be the magic elixir that drives authenticity, while, at the same time, gives brand voices authority and authenticity?

To start with, let's agree on a definition of Native for the purposes of this exploration. There's a technical definition: "A specific mode of monetization that aims to augment user experience by providing value through relevant content delivery in-stream,"[11] but that definition seems a bit too cold and mechanical to capture the zeitgeist of the Native opportunity. There's the philosophical definition: Content that comes from an advertising but that provides as much editorial value as the content that is is integrated with. And, of course with the source clearly labeled. Then, there's the growing trend of publishers taking over creative and turning advertiser needs into destination-specific Editorials.

Each of these definitions suffers from the same problem, as the Web continues to evolve into larger and larger collections of narrow-niche content sites, any Native strategy that requires original content created on a site-by-site basis faces economic challenges that get harder over time as the volume of content on the Web increases. The cost of content creation may not go up, but its relative value decreases in a sea of noise.

Perhaps the best definition so far has come from Jay Rosen, the NYU journalism professor and media thinker. Said Rosen in a tweet, "Proper definition of 'Native' advertising that is as worth reading as the Editorial into which it is mixed, from which it is distinguished."[12] This of course begs the question: does Native advertising need to be mixed with independent Editorials or can brands become curators and storytellers in their own rights.

So, let's look at three examples of how brands are embracing Native and how curation is driving that trend.

IBM - The big blue curator

It used to be that company communication was all top down; messages were 'pushed down' from the C suite to the cubes and employees. Missions were proclaimed. Messages were delivered. Employees and partners were fed the party line. Today, the tools and networks for communication have been broken wide open.

Within the world of corporate communication, two schools of thought exist. There are those who say clamp down: no tweeting without authorization, no posts, no photos and no messaging outside of the approved channels. Then there are those thinkers who are looking to turn this big, noisy mess into value for their brands and corporate parents.

However, you may be surprised to learn just how quickly the tide is turning. As Ben Edwards, the VP of digital strategy and development for IBM, explained: "We're 470,000 people. We made this historical shift from hardware and software to hardware, software and services. We have 30,000 business consultants. We have 3,000 IBM researchers out in the field with the clients and we think employees want to connect and share – that's how work is done."[13]

Historically, communication professionals 'manufactured' official IBM content by the official communicators and pushed it out to the employees and the public.

Edwards is a communicator who looks forward, not back. He explained: "I think there are some emerging roles, potential roles for, you know, coms professionals to think about. One of them I think a lot about is this notion of curation."

At IBM, the voice of the company is increasingly coming from the intranet, known internally as W3. W3 has been leading a transformation from professional to user-generated content within IBM. Mark Ragan, of Ragan Communications, interviewed Edwards on corporate communications and curation.

According to Edwards, "We had 260,000 registered users to that product [W3] internally in 2009 and, between them, they created 600,000 webpages." [14] To put that in perspective, IBM.com has 4.2 million pages, created over 15 years, making it one of the largest corporate sites in the world. In one year alone, IBM employees created 600,000 webpages.

The IBM vision is to embrace, rather than ignore, the growing voice and knowledge of their community. "One of the measures that we like to talk about is called 'Professionally Produced Content versus Employee Published Content' and if I had a graph to show you and put up in a wall here, what you [would] see is the employee-generated content follows an exponent like this and it's probably about 10 to 15 times the volume of [the] professionally-produced content. Professionally-produced content grew, has topped out, and is actually about to go into absent volume; it's about to go into decline. We think we have a role in bringing the external perspective into the employee base," said Edwards. This statement makes IBM a curator as much as a communicator.

At the same time, IBM is driving its brand marketing with a powerful program called Smarter Planet. Smarter Planet is a corporate initiative of the information technology company IBM. The initiative seeks to highlight how forward-thinking leaders in business, government and civil society around the world are capturing the potential of smarter systems to achieve economic growth, near-term efficiency, sustainable development and societal progress.[15] At a time when most marketers were using their dollars to tout their name, IBM's CMO had a very different idea.[16] Jon Iwata said, "Let's embrace a vision and a story rather than tout our brand." The year was 2008 and tech was in a free fall, but IBM looked toward the future and said, "Let's build a Smarter Planet." Iwata explained it this way: "We saw that the combination of instrumentation, interconnectivity and computer intelligence had created an unprecedented opportunity to make the world work better. We initiated a global conversation about the possibilities."

Today, the trends that underpinned Smarter Planet are ubiquitous. Big Data, mobile and cloud are driving innovation across the planet. So, IBM is creating Native content in the form of video stories under the banner "Made with IBM." IBM is producing 50 stories of transformational journeys through the voices of the people who have taken them.

Said Iwata: "We are changing the way we communicate about the exciting possibilities before us – and, at the same time, we are challenging ourselves to deepen the way we engage with our clients."

IBM deployed camera crews and journalists around the world to interview people on the front lines of business – from developers to CEOs, as well as a few IBMers. The crews set out to record stories and explore ideas. From this journalistic reporting came the ideas, words and imagery from which the stories were created; not from an ad agency or a white board, but from exploration in the real world. Some of the stories come from the New York Genome Center, Wimbledon, the Point Defiance Zoo, Blizzard Skis and Memorial Sloan Kettering Hospital. By listening to their customers and telling their stories, IBM is both creating content and building their credibility as a source of Native content.

But going even further is GE, who's embracing content curation as a core Editorial resource.

GE: Media Brand?

GE is publishing a new site with a focus on issues and policy news. The site, Pressing[16] (http://www.gepressing.com), is presented by GE and provides "unique views on policy from the best in news."[17] Its content partners include VOX, CNN,

Politico, NBC News, Slate and Fox News. Pressing also includes Editorials created by Atlantic Media. The site is managed by Rebel Mouse, a publishing platform.

GE is also pushing ahead with other curated content initiatives. GE Capital has launched Pulse, a news site focused on mid-sized companies. Slate pitched the idea and manages the site with content from Slate, Business Insider and *USA Today*. Alexa Christon, GE's manager of global media, said that it's about a conversation, not a POV. "It's really about raising that national conversation, right, left, center," she said.

Curated Content hubs are taking hold giving brands an opportunity to engage in a dialog with their customers. Marketers using curation include Dell with Tech Page One, Xerox with "Real Business" and American Express with "Open Forum."

Rebecca Lieb of Altimeter Group says partnering with quality publishers gives brands a leg up as they become curators. "The number one issue for companies in doing branded content is actually coming up with the content," said Lieb. Quality publishing sources "keep the creative bar relatively low."

Chapter 3: Consumer Voices. Can You Curate Conversation?

When you think of TOM's Shoes, community may not be the first thing that comes to your mind, but it should.[18] In 2006, Blake Mycoskie was inspired to launch "tomorrow's shoes" – known as TOMS. For every pair of shoes you purchase from TOMS, another pair is given away to a child in need. "TOMS is based on giving shoes in a sustainable way, on a one-to-one basis," Zita Cassizzi, TOM's chief digital officer, told MediaBistro.[19]

The TOMS' marketing strategy has five key points:

1. Connecting with the community

"Current and potential customers, mostly millennials, expect an immediate connection from the company," said Cassizzi. The brand favors digital vs. traditional marketing. "We rely on digital, word-of-mouth and 'mocial,' or mobile and social."

Mocial = Mobile and Social. Love that.

For TOM's "giving trips," they connect with NGOs and TOMS has opened retail locations in L.A. and Austin "to add another community connection."

2. Offering multidimensional content

"We deliver products and services, so our content should be relevant and have value, both extrinsic and intrinsic," explained Cassizzi. "At our stores, you feel like you're on a giving trip." TOM's connects with customers' user-generated content (UGC) video and photo contests, inviting customers to share inspirational stories. The top voted user submissions get the customers invited on a giving trips.

3. Building customer relationships for life

"We establish a tone as a best friend, one who's humble and honest, and we provide inspirational quotes," said Cassizzi. "We also focus on service and imbue our brand values in all our efforts." The results is a connection with the customer that reaches beyond the brand and connects on a human level.

4. Continuing the conversation

"TOMS' social media cycle involves listening, reaching out and adapting the conversation accordingly," explained Cassizzi. TOMS empowers customers to act, hosting a yearly "day without shoes," to highlight the issues that face kids without shoes. It's powerful consumer engagement.

5. Creating a culture of innovation

TOMS is growing – expanding its consumer connection beyond shoes to eyewear and coffee. In each case, there's a tie-in with local needs, turning an active consumer community into a curated call to action.

However, the way in which the brands talk and listen to curated consumers isn't simply plug and play. Ben Ayers, the head of social media at Carat, said brands need to get savvy about the types of social interactions they try to create online. [20] "Communities of interest are tremendously powerful, but you've got to have a reason to talk to them," said Ayers. "Brands must create something of value for the user to earn that user's attention. This could mean providing a piece of entertainment or a specific tool or service. The key is being useful."

When it comes to Curated Conversations, the single most important thing for brands to learn is how to stop talking and start listening, which it turns out, is harder than you might think.

As Adobe's curated site CMO.com explained, consumers' embrace of social media means that, for brands, listening online is critical in regard to gathering insights to drive marketing strategy, operations, budget allocation, and products and services.[21] It's not simply having a few interns keeping an eye on Twitter and Facebook; the speed of conversations is moving too quickly across too many social channels. Monitoring and curating social conversations is now a sophisticated software process - and one that's growing. No longer is this a desk in the corner; live, real-time listening posts are now part of brands' 24/7 real-time media operations.

Here are five examples.

1. MasterCard

At MasterCard, they've built a "Conversation Suite," which is their social media command center. There's a massive 40-foot

LED display showing the brand's social conversations in real time. The monitoring tech is Web-based, so any MasterCard employee can engage it. The Conversation Suite analyzed about 85,000 conversations online before MasterCard's announcement of the MasterPass digital wallet at Mobile World Congress in 2012. The knowledge garnered from the active listening helped MasterCard's strategy around the announcement, turning a curated conversation into actionable knowledge.

2. Gatorade

The Gatorade Mission Control Center is based at the company's Chicago HQ. It sits inside marketing, allowing the brand to hear what's being said about Gatorade and related topics (and competitors) around the clock.

Mashable toured the command center and found it to be a remarkable listening post. Mashable reported that Gatorade was able to increase engagement with its product education (mostly video) by 250% and reduce its exit rate from 25% to 9% percent. For big events, the command center shifts into a war room, giving marketers the speed and agility to respond to social media in real time.

3. Adobe

Adobe's social media command center is called "The Customer Listening Post." The center brings together a wide variety of customer access points, creating transparency around the customer experience. Adobe teams can access the voices of their customers, analyze the information to form actionable conclusions and determine which actions have the greatest impact at key points in the customer experience. The Listening Post plays a significant role in Adobe's ability to analyze, assess and act on opportunities for continuous experiential improvements.

4. American Red Cross

For the American Red Cross, social listening happened just recently. Since the organization needs to be able to react quickly in an emergency, the team found that they needed to have their ear to the digital ground. To this end, they built a social media command center in 2012.

Using the command center during the tornadoes in the Midwest gave the Red Cross team members the tools necessary to figure out where to send aid workers. Then they went further, using heat maps see spikes and themes in social conversations and modify their responses based on that knowledge. The social media command center allowed the

Red Cross to deploy food, water, shelter and counseling to the areas that needed it most.

5. Edelman Digital

With a tinge of military precision, Edelman calls its command center the SICC or Social Intelligence Command Center. The SICC was built for Edelman clients who may not need a full-time listening post, but want to be able to ramp up their social information gathering when an event or crisis warrants it. Edelman listens to what the online community says about its clients and then uses that data and its subsequent analysis to plan content strategy, creation, aggregation and Native content creation.

Chapter 4: Global vs. Local

I t seemed so clear that the Web would create what Marshall McLuhan promised would be a 'Global Village' back in 1962, long before there was any thought of the Internet. But trends may be pushing Global back to local. These include increasing use of GPS and other devices, an understanding of the environmental costs of shipping goods around the world, and the growth of the 'buy local' movement Will digital goods and services go 'global' in the curated cloud, while physical goods and services go 'local'? Seth Godin says that's the clear future. But others aren't so sure.

In 2012, the OECD (Organization for Economic Co-operation & Development) along with Boston Consulting Group conducted a study that examined how the Internet is shaped by local forces around the world. Surveying 46 countries, they looked at wireless subscriptions and how businesses, consumers and government use the Internet. Their results showed that different countries have varying Internet economies.[22]

At the time of the study, Britain had the highest consumer spending online per person while Hong Kong was ranked first in connectivity yet the majority of people spent their money offline. Paul Zwillenberg, Managing Director of BCG, predicted an Internet composed of "hundreds of flavors" speculating that it will resemble a branched-off, locally-driven structure rather than one large global network.[23]

In a 2012 press release, BCG announced their report, "The Internet Economy in the G-20." In the report, Zwillenberg underscored the importance of businesses embracing the Internet as a vehicle for economic growth, particularly in developing markets. Countries whose businesses engaged with online consumers resulted in a 22 percent higher growth than those countries with limited Internet presence over a three-year period.[24]

Glocalization

Glocalization: Products or services designed to benefit a local market while at the same time being developed and distributed on a global level.[25] This terminology somewhat challenges Zwillenberg's "hundreds of flavors" perspective. Which track ecommerce is exclusively taking, global or local, has opened up a complex discussion.

In his blog, Keith Richburg ponders the question: "What is the future of local?" Richburg challenges the purity of the term "local" when companies with brands born and bred locally do business globally and in some cases, rely on the international consumer.[26] He delves into the constructs of the virtual community, communities that are formed online with no roots in the real world where the concept of local is tenuous at best.

Ultimately Richburg is exploring the idea of where the heart of any business lies in the landscape of the Internet. Can a brand's identity be scaled-down to its origins? Does it retain that recognition when its reach extends into foreign territories? A fitting example Richburg uses is General Motors, the nucleus of Detroit's auto industry. Today GM sells more cars abroad with China being their biggest customer.[27] He flips the coin, posing the question from a global perspective: "What are the responsibilities of global brands to local communities?"[28]

How important is Local? Well just take a look at the competition heating up between Amazon and Google. Google's X Laboratory, their secretive development program, is now testing drones that will deliver goods to consumers, a technology Amazon also has in the works.[29] This is an intriguing example of how global brands are thinking about their direct impact on local communities and creative ways to improve services to the customer. '"Self flying vehicles could open up entirely new approaches to moving goods...we want to go out and learn about more situations in which aerial delivery could help people in their daily lives..."[30] says Google.

This partially addresses Richburg's question of a company's responsibility to the local community while connecting with the consumer on a meaningful level.

My friend and colleague Brian Solis discussed drilling down into the "hyperlocal." Solis describes himself as both Digital analyst and anthropologist. He's looking both forward and back. He places emphasis on establishing a presence locally, and views it as a prerequisite for companies with a global reputation. "Localization is king," says Solis with absolute certainty.[31] He presents several examples, one being customer engagement in non-English speaking countries. A 2010 study showed 10-15 times more customer engagement on Facebook when companies invested time and attention in non-English speaking countries than companies who were more restricted to English-speaking hubs. Starbucks and Blackberry specifically were cited in the study as implementing these broadened tactics.[32] Solis goes on to present data taken from Translated.net, a linguistics and translation service, that listed the top 10 countries for ecommerce through 2015, China being number one with an 18% market share of online sales. A graphic illustrating the languages with the highest potential of online sales shows English at 25%, Chinese at about 19%, a clear indicator that global businesses need to be proactive in countries where they have, or are fostering, customer relationships.[33]

Hyperlocal & Online Marketing

In business, it's all about capturing your market and sometimes companies miss the mark when they've attained global appeal. Neglecting the local market can potentially erode a company's viability.

A company's relationship with the customer isn't predicated on a physical presence in a community. Rather demonstrating an awareness about locality and the customer who inhabits it can fulfill that role. "Hyperlocal content marketing allows customers to see you as an authority in matters that they deal with every day," says Rachel Priest in her piece "Hyperlocal Content: The Future of Online Marketing?"[34] Taking the time to actively create awareness around the conditions and concerns of the customer strengthens the customer base as a whole. This comes with the challenge of balancing a global presence with hyperlocal engagement. Priest suggests devoting a block of time and schedule a "Just for Locals Day" to cater to the micro-community. She also offers doubling up on marketing content where a business can publish and specialize globally-focused content for the local realms.[35]

Staying locked in to the narrower markets is something companies must include in their arsenal according to today's analysts. However, the counter-argument offers an equally compelling word of caution: narrowing the focus can create unintended consequences depending on the venue.

In 2007, AOL developed "The Patch," a digital newspaper that was heavily focused on news stories at the micro level and specialized Editorial content. Some have argued that AOL's hulking trademark diluted The Patch's purity of product, or focus, as a news source.

Media consultant Leela de Krester commented that The Patch was a casualty of getting "too big too soon" before they could "define their Editorial voice." In 2013, AOL sold off its interest in the site, selling operational control to Hale Global.[36]

Curation plays a critical voice in finding authentic voices for large national and multi-national brands to plug in to local culture. AOL's Patch experiment may have been early, but the opportunities that were driving it were very much on target. Using the Internet as a vehicle to advertise a product or service to a wide *and* narrow market and its cumulative effect plays a delicate role in the complex structures of ecommerce.

Where segmented, localized marketing continues to have success is within the online cable and TV programming. Netflix is the crowning example of developing original, homegrown content that cements a company brand. By and large, Netflix is known for its original content with shows like *House of Cards* and *Orange is the New Black.* Ted Sarandos, Chief Content Officer announced the company plans to acquire a studio to support and sustain Netflix's increasing volume of original programming.[37]

Sarandos said they're rapidly churning out original content while ensuring they maintain quality. Original content is what augments that quality and is the defining element of the Netflix brand, while the industry-driven content - movies, documentaries and TV series - is secondary.

Netflix is headed full-steam into the future and has proclaimed itself as the world's leading Internet TV Network. [38] In the global sphere, Netflix is looking to distribute 10-20% of its local content in overseas markets.[39] The Netflix model is a proven, marketable formula where viewers have more options in the on-demand era of content. Netflix customer-friendly, "localized", marketing methods include personalized content suggestions based on viewers' recent program views.

The simple fact is – the Global vs. Local argument doesn't have a black and white answer. It's both. For things where location matters, where proximity matters, and where regional flavor adds value – local will win the day. But for things where knowledge is the driver – a globally connected world will give Web-connected users a broader network of resources. For both local and global, curation will be key since having wider access to resources by its nature demands a human filter to help discover and surface value and quality.

Simply put – the world is getting bigger... and smaller... at the same time.

Chapter 5: Big vs. Small

Since the advent of television, media has driven the world toward bigness. Larger companies, national and even international brands, and prices have decreased as scale increased, but the cloud has given companies, large and small, shared shelf space in the digital world. So in a cloud powered world, the sameness of big brands starts to run up against the originality and uniqueness of small, focused, target brands.

Modern era marketing is much like a living organism with tendencies, habits and even a life cycle, the nature of which is always changing and in the modern age of technology, the change has never been more dramatic.

In a time when consumers are being inundated with marketing banter, it's becoming increasingly difficult to stand out with your unique message. Consumers demand more from their marketers now than ever before and for the first time in history, they control the ebb and flow of marketing messages. This, in large part, is due to the popularization of the Internet and its associated trends.[40] While consumers are on the winning side of this dynamic new industry, small business are now learning to level the playing field with their larger competitors.

A certain sense of egalitarianism has taken hold and is breathing new life into smaller industry players.

Before the Internet became the sophisticated super power that it has gradually evolved into, the classic marketing technique was to white out all your opposition by dominating the 3 major media sources: TV, print and radio.[41] Large companies could stand out with their messages to consumers because they would habitually flood the same sources with the same messages, ensuring that the consumer never becomes familiar with any sort of alternative messaging.

Indeed, it's a great plan but one that creates a big problem: cost.

As it is in most industries, paying for advertising is incredibly expensive and is subject to a myriad of different purchasing conditions. Certain forms of media can only be purchased in blocks of time and can also be subjected to waiting periods before submissions can be approved. It's a restrictive policy which hinders the ability of any company to customize their message in an effort to reach out to varying demographics.

The expense associated with this style of marketing is massive and the reality was that only big companies could afford to compete in this manner.[42] However with the introduction of online content-based marketing, a new and fresh concept when addressing the history of marketing, the game has changed.

What makes content marketing so revolutionary is that it is essentially free. The size or budget of your company is now a non-factor and consumers have been eating up the concept.

Consumers flock to this new style because it is refined to their needs and can even be manipulated on an hourly basis. This new form of freedom in marketing has given a voice to smaller companies and allowed them to escape the burden of traditional, costly advertising methods.

In essence, they've created a brand new channel, unlike any ever seen before in marketing history, which allows a company to create and maintain a sales relationship with each and every one of its customers. [43] It is truly an unparalleled time in corporate accessibility and has once again granted consumers a way to impact industry without using their wallets.

Creativity is the new currency in content marketing and while larger companies will always have access to better resources, smaller companies can stand out with one simple idea that consumers embrace and attach themselves to through social media and other outlets.

That feeling of intimacy with a company's corporate vision is what consumers want and they cannot achieve that feeling through TV, radio or print media. Factor in the ability for a message to go viral in online terms, and you could be sitting on the most cost-effective form of advertising per impression in human history. This concept would have been deemed foolish no more than 10 years ago and the future could hold an infinite amount of possibilities. [44] Companies are experimenting with database management and different marketing techniques daily through content-creation-based marketing and the results continue to be impressive.

The playing field has truly been leveled.

Big companies no longer host any sort of advantage in online marketing and budgets are now almost a non-factor when compiling a marketing plan. Content marketing has revolutionized the way that people consume marketing messages by demanding richness, substance and applicable value vs petty jingles and repetitious jargon.[45]

Take a look in the mirror. Then look at your customers. You need to be big enough to have authority, and small enough to have intimacy and direct connection to you audience. Curated content can be the glue that gives big brands an honest voice and an authentic POV.

The trend is clear: meet with your consumer one-on-one, on their level, and you will reap the benefits of a cost-effective message which is easily retained and shared. While access to resources and fluid capital will always be an advantage, it is no longer a catalyst to what would now be called an archaic method of marketing. Any size company with any set of resources can participate, be relevant, and most importantly, be successful in this brand new trend.

Part 2

Curation, The Rules of the Road

"Ideas are the most valuable thing... curation is that means to the end."

Peter Hopkins

Chapter 6: Are You A Curator? Should You Be One?

You've purchased this book or it's been given to you, so it would be easy to assume that you've already made the jump and decided that you want to be a curator. However, not so fast. Let's walk you through a simple checklist of curator attributes and see if you fit the bill.

Are you a maker?

Do you create content of some sort – either in short or long form? Are you a writer, poet, painter, songwriter, composer, sculptor, journalist, blogger or author? If the answer is yes, then bravo – you've got one of the critical things that all curators need. A voice. A passion to create. To find unusual linkage and eye-opening connections.

Curation is the art of creating something new, coherent and meaningful out of an abundance of related information and ideas. The reason why there's no such thing as 'machine curation' or 'algorithmic curation' is that curation, at its core – is an artistic and a human endeavor. So, if you see curation as an extension or expansion of your creative voice, then you're in the right place.

Are you a leader?

Curation is the art of standing in the front of the room and telling an audience to follow you. You need to be bold, charismatic, fearless and willing to take risks and make mistakes. Great curators will see around corners, embrace and expose unusual and unexpected themes and sources, and make bold predictions about their passions and beliefs. There's little room for timid, cautious, slow moving curators. The Web operates in real time and curators need to promise their fans and followers that they'll burn the midnight oil to find what's new and notable and get it validated, curated, contextualized and published *first*.

Do you thrive and explore across media boundaries? The ideal curator is multi-disciplinary, willing to forage for ideas and wisdom in tweets, Tumblr posts, LinkedIn pages, Flickr images, Slideshare accounts, Facebook posts, G+ Groups and the legion of emerging voices and sources. The tools are ever changing. The nature of the ideas and the shape of their containers is morphing daily. Vine and Instagram videos have empowered a whole new class of creators. Pinterest boards are now part of the curatorial mix. YouTube, Vimeo and Metacafe are the tip of the video iceberg.

Your fans and friends don't have the time or tools to go spelunking for content in the dark and unexplored corners of the Internet. If they've chosen you as their curator of choice, then they've deputized you to go exploring for them. That means always being hungry for what's next and what's new, wherever it may reside.

Are you a list maker?

Curators are more than hunter/gatherers. They are organizers. They bring order to chaos by creating a framework and then presenting their curated output in a coherent and logical frame. If you've found a thousand potential Editorial elements for a curated page on a sporting event, breaking news story or complex medical or social subject, then the art of honing it down to a digestible, coherent arrangement of Editorial elements is often painfully difficult.

In many ways, the old world of physical limitations, such as the pages in *The New York Times* or the 30 minutes of *The Evening News,* made the need to edit and make brutal cuts a requirement. The limits of that world demanded a firm Editorial hand, but, in the new digital world, it's easy to say "why not let the audience have all of it?" That's a weak excuse and the mark of a curator who is simply a collector of digital bits. The art is in the edit, cutting the avalanche of information into a focused, meaty, revealing curated collection.

Your place or mine?

In the olden days, by which I mean five years ago, Web publishers were all about luring their audiences back to their home (pages). That was where they could grow traffic, monetize visitors and keep return visit numbers growing. That model is gone. Whamo. Now, audiences have settled in to their own consumption patterns, so, for a curator worth his salt, the answer to the question, "Your place or mine?" needs to be a resounding BOTH.

Is your curated content ready to be seen and shared on Facebook? It needs to be. Can visitors tweet it, post it, link to it, email it and share it in any and all ways? Good. What if they want to come and explore the content within your walls – your site? They should be welcome there as well. Content curators are distributors and presenters. They take their collections and their voice out into the world, sharable and mobile, and are happy when audience members consume and share, in any way, what they've created.

Do you have a voice?

Ok, this question is a tricky one. What if you're a curator in a modest field? What if you curate fine art, early childhood parenting or a cancer survivors' group. It's easy to ask curators to have a bold, spunky voice in an Editorial space about video games or adventure sports, but your voice needs to match both your audience's expectations and your own personal brand. You must have a voice that is distinct and memorable. You must break through the clutter and noise and give your readers something to hang their hat on. This statement doesn't mean that you need to blog or even comment on what you curate. Maybe it's the headlines, maybe it's your Twitter voice. However, if your fans and followers think that you're just a collection of links, then someone whose voice connects with them is going to romance your audience away.

Let's be clear about one thing: having a voice will mean that some people will find it not to their liking. That's the trade-off of having something to say – some folks will disagree with you. However, if you don't have a voice, then you're not a curator with a long-term game plan. In a world of information abundance, the clarity and focus of your curatorial vision and voice is imperative. You don't need to have a voice today, but you do need to be excited about embracing your emerging voice and taking some risks along the way.

Do you have a gut for finding/filtering?

Curators are constantly searching – exploring, searching and ruthlessly discarding.

In the world of separating signal from noise, you need to be willing to expose yourself to the relentless din of signal and be able to make snap judgments, often without regard for the granular accuracy of each individual curatorial cleave.

Imagine if you were the curator at the Museum of Modern Art, MOMA. You'd arrive with a Ph.D. in Art History, you'd have a deep understanding of your craft and the art that you'd have at your fingertips to curate would, for the most part, have already been discovered, engaged with and embraced by numbers of critics, artists and historians. However, digital content curators has no such organic process to help them narrow their field of vision.

Often the phrase 'curation' is used with the image of a fire hose and that image is apt. Digital curators are faced with a fast-moving, raw, unfiltered stream of information. Some information is from trusted sources and the mainstream media, but much of it from unknown makers and anonymous Tweets and posts. What is accurate? What is not? The curator needs to balance authentic sources with voices and points-of-view outside the mainstream. The rare Editorial content is often the most provocative, but, also, the most risky. Managing this balance is a core curatorial skill to be honed and advanced.

What about your members? Do they get a say?

If curators have a strong voice and POV, then how do they deal with audience engagement and participation? This question is another interesting conundrum for the modern curator. Audiences want to participate; they want to be engaged and listened to. A strong curator is both a leader and listener. Curators invite participation, encourage their engaged community to suggest content, help shape Editorial direction and participate in often-frothy debates and discussions. The nature of curation extends beyond the content as curators curate their members as well. Valuable members with strong points-of-view and real insight into the category or community are a treasure to be embraced and encouraged. Outspoken members who make the community less welcoming or downright hostile need to be marginalized or even removed. It's a tricky balancing act to foster open participation, but set clear guidelines and community standards. However, if you can't lead with both content and community, then you're just waiting for the moment when the center of gravity changes.

Can you mix?

Have you ever tended bar, spun records or set up a photo exhibit at a gallery? If so, good because, when you get right down to it, curators are mixologists. They are tastemakers who specialize in taking elements that may, in fact, be available to others and creating a collection that contains a unique vision and voice. The mix is essential. Add a bit of humor and you may make magic. Overdose on raucous comedy and you may lose the useful balance you set out to achieve. There's no handbook for your mix; it's yours, but be conscious of the fact that a mix is more than a handful of related items set side-by-side. If you've ever had a great Martini or gone to dance club where the DJ was on fire – you know that getting the mix right can make all the difference.

There's a temptation to think that, in a crowded marketplace of content, you can have more impact by creating break-out content. However, I'd make the argument that whether you're teaching, entertaining or enhancing your topic, curating content is to your advantage. Why? Being a useful filter makes you a destination rather than a source of content. Helping your audience by being a resource of valuable content makes you more than a voice in the wilderness. By aggregating and curating a wide variety of sources, you become the keeper of the coherent flame, a unique and valuable resource.

The volume of noise in the world makes a curator's role as an identifier of trends into an important voice. The shift from delivering 'facts' to discerning patterns is a growing and important one.

By framing the conversation rather than contributing to it, you're providing a unique and valuable resource, context. Agencies call this 'thought leadership' and it's highly valuable.

There's no doubt that audiences are hungry for clarity. As I've said before, viewers don't want more content, they want less. They want highly useful and focused collections.

Curation moves you from a voice in the noise to a leadership role. Curation allows you to define the focus of a conversation and set the tone. Having a defined POV is critical for successful curators.

Defining yourself as the ultimate arbiter of what is important and what is not makes you the decision-maker, the central point of power. Your readers and viewers only have so much time to consume content, so your role as the smart filter builds audience loyalty.

Chapter 7: The Editorial Function

Within the world of print, there's a temptation to suggest that calling someone a 'curator' is just a newfangled word for 'Editor' but that isn't right. Let's explore for a bit what the Editorial function is – and where it diverges from the role of the curator.

Anytime there's a blog post or an article about curation, someone pipes up in the comments with a weary sigh and says: "Isn't this just a fancy new word for an Editor?"[46]

So, let's deal with this in a direct way.

A curator is NOT an Editor. Here's why.

Editors come in many shapes and sizes. The flavors include Acquisitions Editor, Articles Editor, Assignment Editor, Assistant Editor, Associate Editor, Contributing Editor/Editor At-Large, Department/Features Editor, Executive Editor, Managing Editor, and Editor-in-Chief.

What none of these titles include is curator.

Editors provide a critical skill for refining and improving content that is created by a professional writer to a professional outlet.

The word "Editor" gets used across a number of related fields – all related to content.

You can find Editors in books, both fiction and non-fiction, as well as magazines, newspapers, films and video. Editors touch content – clarifying, polishing, and making sure that the author has a clear story and narrative. Often the Editor cuts out material, bringing clarity to an audience. In most cases Editors are called on to make sure material fits in the space and time allowed.

Articles have to hit word count target, films need to fit into allotted time. But the effort of different Editors can span from hours to months. Film and book Editors work on long timelines, while newspaper Editors may have little time to get an article ready. Web Editors almost always work against a ticking clock.

Even within disciplines, the definition of Editor varies. Within journalism, the role can be as broad as Editor-In-Chief, who oversees the Editorial voice of an entire publication.

The Managing Editor works under the EIC, and directs writers - either staff or freelance – to produce content. The Copy Editor is focused on facts, checking to make sure articles are accurate and grammatically correct.

In publishing, the title 'Editor' takes on an entirely different role. Acquisition Editors are responsible for finding talent – authors and manuscripts that fit the publishers imprint.

At some publishers, the Acquisition Editor will 'own' the author from contract through to publication – but often they author is handed off.

A Development Editor will work directly with the writing – managing the authoring process. And a Copy Editor at a publishing house will work with the finished manuscript to make sure it is factual, grammatically correct, and meets the particular imprint's style guide.

While Editors are hands on, curators tend to live above the content creation layer. And while Editors tend to be behind the scenes, curators are increasingly bringing a voice and a POV that often impacts the sources of curated content and the context in which it's presented.

While Editors may bring knowledge and skills that a writer might not have, curators are at arm's length from content creators. Curators are creating new Editorial collections from finished work, making limited adjustments to headlines or thumbnails, but not editing within the body of the work. Curators are 'creators' in a way that Editors are not.

A curator's job is to create logic and meaning in collection of content, to create an Editorial flow that provides context and meaning. Curators are responsible to their audiences, while Editors often have a split loyalty to both audience and author.

"An Editor is a mediator. She stands between the writer and the reader and helps them to understand each other," says the Writers' Helper blog.

Curators are in many ways creators

At least the good ones are. Think of a disc jockey at a night club. They all start with the same raw material: songs. Some DJ's create what we can all agree are new works-using the music to create re-mixes, mashups, and new songs. The artist "Girl Talk" certainly goes in that category.

Curators create entirely new Editorial experiences by finding sources from diverse and sometimes divergent points of view.

Curators come with an Editorial objective, a POV, and their own Editorial voice. Sometimes curators are both writers and gatherers. Other times, curators will use their contextual POV and perspective to organize material in a way that collectively creates a larger story.

So the Editor's job is to refine and improve Editorial that is authored by others. Curators ARE authors in their own right.

So, if Editors refine a topic, and curators define a topic, why does it matter now?

Because we live in an era of Editorial abundance. Everyone with a keyboard, a camera, and a phone is creating 'Editorial'—bits and pieces of what is often a larger story. Curators who can filter the meaningful content from the fire hose of data provide readers with both context and a richer Editorial experience.

My conclusion is that Editors remain essential, but their role is unchanged. Curators are something new, and needed. Filtering the deluge of data-finding meaning from the maelstrom-is a new and essential role.

Yuri Milner - the Russian Internet investor whose firm has invested in Facebook, Groupon, and Zynga, now says the next space he's looking at is curation, "With the number of sources, and doubling of information every 18, 24 months. I think the next big thing is curation."

Milner's made some smart calls, so unless he starts investing in Editors, I'd say curation is a safe bet.

Chapter 8: The Legal / Moral Questions

O k, at first blush – content curation feels weird. And so it's not hard to understand why people ask, "Can I really do that?" Fair question. Can you use other people's content as the basis for your curation? It's worth remembering that the law tends to lag behind social and industry trends, so there is both the letter of the law and then actual best practices that are emerging as industry standards.

Copyright, Fair Use, and Ethics

For the purposes of this section, I'll address them both with the understanding that a small site, a startup, or community site is going to be more comfortable on the outer edge of practices, while large companies, media companies who control large swaths of content assets, or anyone who looks to a potentially litigant as a 'deep pocket' is going to probably land on the more conservative side of the fence. Your comfort level is only something you can determine.

Curation is a three-legged-stool, with content creator, the curator, and the consumer all having a say in how attention and value is divvied up.

The Creator

This is the content maker. If the maker works for a large company, then they have an economic agenda. They are looking to create visibility for their brand, and may well be providing content with some sort of advertising built in to the feed. If they are a smaller creator, then they are less likely to have monetization, but more likely to want to build brand value. In either case, they are going to probably want to be part of your curation mix, as long as you play fair.

The curator

That's you. You're looking to find the best of the best, to present it to your audience, and to help give a particular post or link traffic or value. And, yes – you want your audience to find value in your mix, so you're building brand value here as well.

The Consumer

They're the folks who count on you to find, organize, and share the best of the best. They're choosing you because they want your mix. If one of your sources was a better fit, they'd be going to them. They've made their choice.

Here are 10 BEST PRACTICES to follow, with good judgment of course:

1. Excerpt, Don't Lift

Making the content your own matters. So taking a portion of a post or article. Don't cut and past the whole thing. That's stealing. However, there are a few exceptions. Twitter, 140 characters is the whole thing, but less probably doesn't make sense. And video: embeds are, if you're getting them from an approved source (not a scrape) expected to be used in their entirety.

2. Attribution.

Giving the credit to the creator is both good karma and the right thing to do. Heck, it's what you'd want when someone curates your work.

3. Context.

Providing useful context around curated material is important, and editorially essential. But that doesn't mean that context can be achieved simply by providing related material from other sources. Remember, your audience came to you for your POV, and this single piece of content is only valuable to your audience if you provide the relevant related material and commentary.

4. Link back – because.

Because it's nice. Because it's fair. Because your visitors may want to see the Editorial in its natural environment. Only you can decide how to present links, but don't leave them out.

5. Images.

Read the fine print. Whenever possible, use advanced search in Flickr, Bing, or Google Images to find images with CC marks, creative commons. If not, consider using thumbnails and linking back to larger images. But using copyright images at full size is asking for trouble.

6. No-Follow is a no-no.

The no-follow attribute steals SEO credit from the source; it's simply not nice. Don't do it.

7. An Excerpt Is an Excerpt.

It needs to be proportionally small, meaning if the article you're reposting from is 6 pages, then the excerpt should be a paragraph or two. You want to summary and point, not lift and steal.

What about Fair-Use?

This is one of those things that's pretty hard to define. For some publishers, fair use is a clear definition. It's somewhat clear for breaking news, less clear for other uses.

Here's what my friend and fellow curator, Pawan Deshpande of Curata, says about fair use:[47]

Fair-use and curation of other people's content becomes an issue when it's not handled properly because the interest of the curator and the publisher overlap significantly. They both want a piece of the same pie: site traffic, increased SEO and visitor retention. When the curation is done wrong, the curator's interests are served but the publisher sees no benefit. But if it's done properly, in a symbiotic manner that makes it a win-win, curation can serve the interest of the publisher, the curator, and ultimately the audience.

Here's what the law says about Fair Use and the four considerations that factor into it:

Section 107 contains a list of the various purposes for which the reproduction of a particular work may be considered fair, such as criticism, comment, news reporting, teaching, scholarship, and research. Section 107 also sets out four factors to be considered in determining whether or not a particular use is fair.

The purpose and character of the use, including whether such use is of commercial nature or is for nonprofit educational purposes

The nature of the copyrighted work

The amount and substantiality of the portion used in relation to the copyrighted work as a whole

The effect of the use upon the potential market for, or value of, the copyrighted work

The distinction between what is fair use and what is infringement in a particular case will not always be clear or easily defined. There is no specific number of words, lines, or notes that may safely be taken without permission. Acknowledging the source of the copyrighted material does not substitute for obtaining permission.

The key pieces here are that you are not hurting the original author by sharing their work, you are not sharing too much of their work, and that simply acknowledging them as a source may not be sufficient.

Pawan's take is clear and concise. But of course, your take may vary depending on where you stand. For example, a large publisher may want to be more conservative about how they define fair use, or risk that others will use a liberal definition in how they use their copyrighted material. Larger companies often have deeper pockets, and therefor are the targets of litigious individuals. The risk here is that companies will chip away at legitimate fair use claims by simply telling their curators or authors that everything need to be licensed.

Perhaps the most authoritative work on this subject is *Reclaiming fair use: How to put balance back in copyright,* by Patricia Aufderheide and Peter Jaszi.[48]

Aufderheide is acknowledged as one of the country's leading experts and a passionate advocate in the field. She heads the Fair Use and Free Speech research project at the Center for Social Media at the School of Communications at American University. She has been a Fulbright and John Simon Guggenheim fellow and has served as a juror at the Sundance Film Festival among others.[49]

For Aufderheide, curators deserve this new-found place in the content ecosystem. "I think curators are in the same class of creative actors as Editors and museum/gallery curators. They know a field of production, they exercise standards, and they use that knowledge and judgment to showcase work in new contexts that add meaning."

Her book is a powerful voice for advocacy. "I think all culture always has been a Remix Culture. The illusion that creators are wholly original in their creations is just that, an illusion. I believe that curators create new material—the collection that they create by selection. This is the most participatory and productive era of cultural expression in the history of the world."

"It is encouraging to see signs of monetizing the work of curation," says Aufderheide. "Monetization will reward higher levels of effort in curation and articulation of Editorial standards. I do not mean that this field of activity needs policing; I mean that there is a very loose notion at the moment of what is involved, and as the activity is elaborated, ways of valuing it will emerge; monetization will be a useful spur."

So, just how important is it that share, remixing, and new works emerge from existing media? "The emergent economy has shareability built into it. At the same time this is and has been a bedeviling moment to be an incumbent media company, especially with bricks/mortar issues—towers, antennas, printing presses, etc." But, the challenges to existing business models notwithstanding, Aufderheide says we're at an exciting and critical crossroads. "Limiting that shareability means crippling one's participation in [the new] economy."

"As monetization of spreadable culture grows, more and more people will become actively interested in their own monopoly rights under copyright, at the same time that they will need their fair use rights to create work. So creators need to know both sides of the copyright balance, because most of us want and need both sides of it," says Aufderheide.

Her video presentation at TEDx Poynter Institute tells the story well here: http://bit.ly/FairUseTEDx.[50]

While this isn't a book about Fair Use (you should read Pat's book for that), there are some basic principles that Aufderheide and the Center for Media and Social Impact share, and they should provide a basic understand of why copyright is not absolute.

What is Fair Use?[51]

Section of copyright law that protects the rights of creators who want to incorporate other people's copyrighted material into their work.

Fair use is in some ways similar to the process of quoting other sources when writing a paper. That's essentially what fair use is: quoting. Generally fair use is using somebody else's work to make a new point or idea.

Why is it Important?

The fair use section of copyright law basically says that if even if I have created a piece of work and it's copyrighted, I don't actually have an ABSOLUTE right to control when and how it's used. There are times when people can use it without my permission.

Why would copyright law allow that?

1st Amendment! Freedom of speech. It's a safety valve to prevent censorship.

Fair use protects the rights of creators to critique existing culture, to take unpopular stances. Fair use also recognizes that we're all "Standing on the shoulders of giants," that is, we're all taking inspiration from, and borrowing and re-purposing pieces of culture that other people have created.

The law identifies four "factors" that should always be considered, although they don't have to have equal weight and they don't need to be the only ones: The nature of the new work, the nature of the original work, the amount of material taken, and effect on the market.

Chapter 9: Impact of curation on SEO

The letters SEO have been known to make webmaster's blood run cold. How can you optimize your sites so that search engines find it? Well, curation plays a critical and complex role in this equation. It used to be that search engines, in particular Google rewarded the creators of original content with the best "page rank" and search results. But now, as content overload impacts the Web, sites that both create and curate are increasingly valuable for SEO results.

Today there exists a general consensus that content curation helps immensely with one's SEO efforts.[52]

We curate content because in this day and age we are all seeking balance. Not all of us have time to read a full, originally-crafted article. We have busy schedules and restraints on time, money and other resources. Therefore, there is a need for current, high quality material that people will want to, and actually have time to, read. This is where content curation comes into play. As many institutions are struggling to keep up with the demand for content, but just do not have the resources to do so, content curation provides a manner in which the most relevant information can be covered, traffic can be increased, and high SEO ranks attained as well.[53]

The five types of content curation...[54]

- aggregation
- distillation
- elevation
- mashups
- chronology

Bruce Clay's study and what it illustrates...

This is perhaps the most well-known piece of data that exists which illustrates the power and efficiency of curated content when it comes to SEO. Bruce Clay, Inc. (BCI) is an Internet marketing optimization company providing search engine optimization (SEO) services, pay-per-click (PPC) advertising management, SEO-friendly Web design and information architecture, and social media and conversion rate optimization services.

Tests were performed to observe how three different combinations of curated and original content fared in terms of search rankings. The first post was formed from summaries that were automatically generated, along with curated links. The second post included 200+ words of unique commentary along with editorialized curation. The last consisted of an actual passage drawn from the original post and links, along with an editorialized curation.[55]

Results: the first combination was found to have dropped significantly in rank (it was essentially duplicate content), while the second dropped in rank only slightly. The third (the one with the most unique content) was able to match the rank of the original post, taking the first spot.[56]

Remember, curated content can indeed help immensely with SEO (and can do so in less time than original...) but one must be sure to apply aspects such as originality, value, relevance etc. (in other words, it must be done correctly.)

Here are keys to successful content curation that will positively affect SEO.

Originality

As found in the study, curated content can work well as long as it is accompanied by enough unique and original content. The average suggestion of original content is 200+ unique words. The more unique your work is, the more likely people are going to return to your site, or share it which will create more traffic...and so on...and so forth...[57]

Sources are of high quality and are diverse in nature

If you are publishing information on the Internet and you are found to be connected to disreputable or unreliable sources, your whole identity and authenticity is at risk. Sourcing reputable sources puts you on their radar and therefore can increase inbound links as they share more and more (and as their readers share more and more!).[58]

Produce a variety of content

This means not just simply copying or sharing the same content over and over again. People want to read about what is fresh, new, and trending, and will share as a result.

Shares are also a good determination of the quality of an article

If you have a good quality article, people will be interested and will be more inclined to share with their social networks.[59]

Your content possesses value

There needs to be enough thought and effort put into the content you are curating. This also relates with the idea of being selective. Content curators need to be skilled at being able separating the useful, trending, and vital information from the rest. Value is essential because it is at the core of why people choose to read your content (and share it!) over the content of others. No one is going to read your article it is not relevant, or valuable to them. In terms of SEO, an article of little value = little views = little shares = poor ranking![60]

Be selective

A great content curator is someone who can easily (and quickly) sort between what relevant, interesting, and valuable information, and what is not. Curated content is very useful in this day and age because a) people do not have the time and resources to produce as much original content as is needed and b) people simply do not have the space in their schedules to read through an entire article. They'd much rather skim a short one for the important bits.

When a site consistently produces relevant curated content, not only do people view it as valuable, but Google views it as relevant and dynamic, making it much more likely to move up in SEO rank.

Google is not being personal when they choose someone's content over yours. They do it because they are solely focused on the value of the product they produce.[61] Therefore, if you work to keep the value readers receive consistent through selectivity and relevance when you curate your content, your SEO will surely benefit.

Building relationships with the sources you draw content from

One can accomplish this using a couple of methods. You might decide to ask permission to use an author's content, or send them a quick email to thank them for it. You can even politely ask them to share it for you (and often times, they are more than happy to do so). Again, more shares = better SEO which equals more traffic and better reach.[62]

How people try to 'cheat' at SEO

Link hoarding. Sometimes webmasters will attempt to retain their SEO rank by using 'no-follow' links. Essentially what this means is they will use another site's content, and in doing so, will gain benefits from the arrangement. However, they set it up in such a way that the original content's site does not receive anything in return. Not only is this unethical but Google will likely track you down and penalize you for link hoarding.[63]

Curating for engine bots, not people. Sometimes people will get the smart idea to try to cheat the system, and attempt to do this by trying to curate content for the search engine bots in order to gain a higher rank. Many of the authors reminds us that it is much better to focus on one's audience when curating content. People who authentically enjoy the information you produce will link back to you, which is far more helpful in SEO than trying to out-game the system by appealing to the bots.[64]

Chapter 10: Curation and Community

While curation is clearly the key to finding coherent content in an increasingly noisy world, a drive also exists to find ways to make curation efficient. The algorithm folks keep looking for a magic way to take your clicks and Web travels and turn them into content discovery robots. However, as you've hopefully concluded by now, the use of these robots don't tend to result in happy content experiences.

Another alternative is to empower the crowd, your audience, and turn their collective interests and content recommendations into community-curated content. Does this work? Can a community actual provide a path to curation? The answer is - maybe. If your community already organizes around a coherent set of ideas and voices, then a collection of recommendations or 'likes' might provide a useful breadcrumb trail to valuable content.

Joe Wikert's take is that community curation can provide value and an economy of scale.[65] Wikert has been involved in the publishing word for many years, as the VP and executive publisher at John Wiley & Sons and, before that, as the general manager, publisher and chair of the prestigious Tools of Change (TOC) conference at O'Reilly Media, Inc. Writing on his blog, "Digital Content Strategies," Wikert said, "With paywalls coming back in style, readers are discovering more brands are clamping down on content access. Whether it's accomplished through metering or subscriber-only access, a day doesn't go by when I haven't run into a paywall. That's OK. There's too much content out there anyway."

Wikert says the problem won't be resolved by limiting content; the problem instead is too much noise. "What I really need is more curation and less volume."

Wikert says that he wants to pay someone to read content and act as a filter – and that concept isn't new to readers of this book. However, he takes it a step further – suggesting that the community can play a role and that newspapers could benefit from this type of curation.

"Let's say you're a newspaper or magazine publisher. Assume for a moment that you're willing to grant full, behind-the-paywall access to community content curators. There are sports experts, business experts, local community experts, etc. These curators are reading everything you're publishing and picking the best of the best, the must-reads for the day/week/month. They in turn publish their lists to a whole new set of subscribers; these readers pay for access to only the content recommended by the curator, not the full editions." Community members are deputized to help filter and organize content.

Wikert sees curation as a way to create a whole new community of engaged members. "The best curators float to the top and drive more subscriptions than the others and you pay them a commission for each subscriber they bring in. curators establish brand names for themselves, as in, 'Hey, if you're into travel, you need to subscribe to Bob Thomas...he finds all the best travel articles so I don't have to.'"

The pricing of a curated service in the Wilkert model would depend on a number of factors, including how much the audience values curation. Wilkert is spot on when he says that, for a professional audience, time equals money. Curated content for a doctor, lawyer any other professional with a high hourly rate could easily pay for community curation and he doesn't think that curated summaries should be cheap just because they're short. "Just because it's shorter doesn't mean it's worth less. In fact, if you're saving me time, I'm willing to pay more, so these summaries, curated by community members, could have a higher price than the original eBook."

Of course, there are a number of sites that already use community curation. The first site in this category was probably Digg.com. Founded in 2004, Digg started out as an advertising-supported site that allowed its community to up vote and down vote ('digg' and 'bury') content submitted by its members, creating the voice of the community. It was almost sold to Google in 2008, but negotiations fell through. A 2010 relaunch was marred by glitches. Disenfranchised Digg users shifted to reddit. The original reddit was launched in 2005 by Alexis Ohanian and purchased by publisher Condé Nast in 2006. In 2008, it went open source and, in 2011, it was spun off, operating as an independent entity (although still owned by Advance Publications, the company that owns Condé Nast).[66]

Today, reddit has over 100 million unique visitors per month, driven by a community curation spirit in which users submit links and then vote them up or down. Those users who submit items of particular interest gain 'karma,' which is a currency of sorts and figures into how well your submissions do. It's basically a measure of how good of a curator you are.

Ava Seave, writing for *Forbes*, was able to find the data behind the practice in a way that makes it all line up.[67] "What we are finding is that the market as a whole is embracing the idea of curation and enabling their users to create thoughtful collections of content," Curalytics founder and product lead Steffon Davis told Seave. "However, while that data is being collected, most companies don't know what to do with that data. They have it now, but they haven't started to unlock it."

New York-based, Curalytics gets raw curation data from customers and gives them back an analysis of "Taste Groups," "Taste Leaders" and other information and related data that can drive the curation functionality for that site. "Within these communities, we analyze time stamps to see who is curating likeable content first," explained Davis. "We call that a 'curator Score.'

So, if a person can consistently curate content that other people end up adding to their collections after them, then they become identified as a Taste Leader. And that information is what a lot of platforms want to know. We enable them to measure them and find them."

"A user can start interacting with the content," explained Davis. "They don't have to follow anyone, they don't have to friend anyone. All they have to do is start interacting with the content on a Web site. It's a way to create community outside of social connections. It's kind of a content first approach to a community."

Curation functionality is appearing across all types of ecommerce and digital publishing sites. Davis noted the types of companies that will benefit most immediately from the community curation analysis are ecommerce companies that have wish lists, or any ecommerce company that has integrated an actual curation functionality that lets people create collections of content, music companies that have playlists and any type of visual platform that has a "gallery" as a metaphor, such as Flickr.

Curation data contains the human, subjective elements that the Internet is missing. "We see there are two types of subjective data. First, there is the 'liking' or the 'thumb-upping,' which, from a data POV, is like a warehouse, and everything they have ever liked is piled up in that warehouse.

But contrast that with curation data, [then] that is a second type of subjective data. It can be much richer. It's like looking into my home and seeing each room of my home and actually contextualize[ing] the content in my life."

To see how taste is 'distributed' is key to understanding your community. "You need to power user analytics so that a site owner can actually see how taste is distributed across the community and start making these informed decisions about how they want to grow their community. And if you can't see how taste is distributed, you can't have that conversation."

The power of your community can be harnessed, amplified and organized around curation. You just need to give members the tools and capture data around behavior to see how leaders are engaging. Curation bubbles up from there.

Chapter 11: Curation and Contextual Relevance

I t's easy to think of curation as little more than selection and organization, but that would miss one of the critical elements, the third 'c', if you will. Context. If the first two c's are collection and creation, then the third c is context. To provide context, curators must have knowledge and understanding of the context of the world for which they are creating. Such knowledge requires an understanding of both the subject matter and the makeup of the audience for which you'll be curating.

In other words, context is critically important. Content curators must adapt their curation skills to the ways people of today's generation consume and interact with information.[68] In *The Role of curation in Journalism*, Mike Masnick talks about the changing face of journalism. However, the points that Masnick makes are relevant for curators on a broader scale.

Masnick explained that journalists simply "re-report" what is already out there and that it is the curators who take the information and make it available and accessible to the people at-large. They are extremely important entities to the success of firms, a point that cannot be overstated However, not all newspapers are prepared to let this happen as they still prefer to be the last word on all topics.[69]

However, it's not just the behavior of creators that is changing; the audience is changing as well. For example, today's news world no longer consists of the unilateral relationship between the news station and audience that was prominent in the past.

Although newspapers, news firms and large news entities still exist, there has been crucial change. News is not only being created by anchors and journalists anymore. Now, news can be made and, in the same vein, disseminated by the average Joe with an iPhone or laptop and a general knowledge of the Internet's social platforms.

This not only makes 'news making' accessible to everyone, but also broadens the horizons on what can actually be considered as newsworthy information (or content). Therefore, institutions need to learn how to adapt to this bilateral and dynamic flow of information creation rather than sticking to their old patterns and missing out on all of the other mediums and platforms available to reach additional audiences.[70]

How do these organizations adapt? Technology. Specifically, with the new technologies and technological devices used to access and interact with the content.[71] It has already been established that content curation works, but if you don't keep in mind the technological context through which your curated information will likely be consumed, then you are at an extreme disadvantage.

For example, in the past, pretty much the only method available to spread news, knowledge and ideas was through the medium of radio, which meant that content needed to be gathered and then adapted for vocal transmission in such a way that it would be understood by the larger public sphere. One thing also to note here is the top-down, authoritative approach to this type of content distribution.

Only one party has the time, resources and authority to gain information, call themselves 'the reputable sources,' and then go on to share this information with the public at-large in a highly non-interactive way (i.e., the news experts tell you what the news is and you simply listen...this is not a two-way street).

Heidi Cohen is both an author and a marketer. After receiving her A.B. with Honors from the University of Chicago and her M.B.A. in Marketing with Honors from NYU's Stern Graduate School of Business, she built her marketing career at well-known brands for major international corporations, such as

Citibank, Bertelsmann and *The Economist*. Cohen has learned how to break complex marketing concepts into easy-to-consume chunks. Writing on her blog, the Actionable Marketing Guide, Cohen particularly emphasized an urgency for institutions to explore new technologies and she gave the example of Google, who is taking on Apple right now.[72] Google is a giant search engine (which we all know), that has moved to a search platform on mobile devices (the dominant one, in fact).

Now, it has the Android system and the Play platform. Google also has YouTube! and a Chromecast device as well. These are all mediums through which content can be curated and this situation shows how far one can reach by making use of the technological age we are in (i.e., paying attention to the current context of our generation and curating accordingly). It also demonstrates how much an institution would limit itself in terms of growth and success if it were only to stick to one platform (e.g., text format) and ignore all others available.[73]

Content curators must have knowledge of their target population's attributes, psyche, likes, dislikes, etc. curators must be aware of the attributes of the particular population for which they are curating (i.e., they must try to be as knowledgeable as possible on the traits, likes, dislikes, personalities, skills, interests and psychological makeup of their audience).[74] Curating great content is good, but it is not enough. Without knowledge of the larger context of the population (i.e., who will actually be consuming this information), it is hardly possible to curate appropriately. What is the point of working to separate and collect pieces of vital information if they are not relevant to the  particular audience on which you are focused?

One final thing to think about is the interaction with content. People will not be inspired or encouraged to share or even read what you have created for them if you haven't compiled it with their needs in mind. In this way, the personal context of the people becomes even more relevant.

The needle in the haystack

As stated before, the Internet in the simplest of descriptions is a mass of information. curators are essential in that they are able to sift through this data to pick out what is relevant, working to provide the most essential and valuable content to the audience on a consistent basis, which allows them to form trusted relationships with their audience (another aspect of context to keep in mind!). One may accomplish this through customization.[75] In other words, what can you provide that is different from all of the other sites and how?[76]

Once an institution has studied the characteristics of the audience it is targeting, it can begin to tailor the content it curates to this audiences' specific needs. This strategy will be the most successful in the long run because it, ultimately, provides more value for what the audience will repeatedly find is consistent, high quality information that they can actually *relate* to because it has been customized for them.

Digital Pulse's article on social shopping[77] gives the example of niche online retail sites, such as Etsy, which are customizable with the context of the audience in mind (i.e., the world of people who are time-constrained and want easy access, but also have certain tastes and preferences when it comes to online shopping).[78] Content curation alone could not accomplish this as one must take the analysis of the context into account. The context provides vital cues by which you can tweak your strategy in order to maximize reach, rank, growth and potential. In addition, once you understand the inner workings of the audience, you can develop ways through which more of your audience can actually be engaged with your site (i.e., find out who these people are in their entirety and customize fully to them).

The larger message here is that if institutions want to be successful, then they have to be willing to adapt to the changing needs and behaviors of the people when it comes to content consumption.[79] They must also be willing to study and learn from them their patterns of action in order to curate the best, most accessible and successful content for them. Ultimately, these aspects will add value and relevance, two important pieces of content curation. There is order to this madness and you can't just expect things to go viral right off the bat.[80]

The experts at Price Waterhouse Coopers (PWC) wrote on their blog, Digital Pulse, four ways you can achieve the right mix of content. It is important to note that all of the strategies keep the context in mind:[81]

1. Strategic integration of content into broader marketing and business plans

How will you actually market this content? You must have knowledge of the surrounding context, the bigger picture.

2. A firm understanding of who your audience is and what types of content engage them.

The audience's make-up, how to best address this, the psychological context and personal context of the audience and how this affects and interacts with the content.

3. Developing a range of multimedia content mediums that are curated specifically for your audience

4. Knowing your audience and how they consume media, what is the context for which this content is being produced? How should it be produced?

Content and context interact on a purely visual level

Understanding how your users engage content can help you raise points, emphasize emotions, solidify arguments and everything in between. As humans are visual in nature, placing the right content in the correct context can give rise to a variety of meanings and emotions. So, in this way, understanding visual context is integral to successful content curation as it allows one to use vision as yet another means of transmitting ideas. For example, without a deeper knowledge of context, one may haphazardly place two articles side-by-side that, in reality, are highly related to each other and could spark a controversial and negative debate (which may have been unintentional) that might ultimately leave your audience viewing your site in a negative light (or maybe even drive them away!). In the same vein, this can also be used in your favor as images, videos and text can be placed together in an appealing manner and be encouraged to work off each other to create a desired effect. For example, filling a page on 'happiness' with articles, pictures and videos that are highly inspiring in nature (and that all complement each other visually) allows you to create a positive mood for the page. Overall, a curator can use this knowledge of context to create a positive mood or vibe in order to affect the audience on a more psychological level.

It all comes down to relationships

Content curation does not exist in isolation. It is ultimately accomplished with the consumer/audience in mind, suggesting that a bilateral relationship exists between the two. One of the challenges of any platform or institution is to create and maintain strong, lasting relationships with its audience. Another challenge is to figure out what the best ways are to keep the audience active and engaged.[82] This point is of vital importance and is the aspect of context that you do not want to forget. How do you create content in the context of your audience, keep providing them with quality information and keep them coming back? Remember that without them, there is nothing! (You cannot have one without the other because they literally feed off each other.) From them, you achieve popularity, loyalty, awareness and reach and, in return, you must provide them with high quality and valuable information all of the time. Therefore, you must keep this in mind and work to cultivate your relationship with them. It is suggested that you try to go above and beyond for your audience and get feedback regularly so that you can tweak your methods accordingly.[83]

Orbit Media has a great list of actionable content curation tips, with a focus on context.[84]

1. **Build a monster list**

    In our visually-oriented culture, the 'everything at once' culture, this drives users to seek more information with less work. In addition, many people would rather look at photos than text as it is much easier and faster to comprehend and is also more appealing.

2. **Develop stellar roundup posts**

    We, as a society, love when others do the work for us (even better is when the content can be trusted and is of high quality).

List formats are short and appealing as they are easy-to-read, fast and efficient, great in the context of our fast-paced world when you only need the most important information and nothing else.

3. Be a namedropper

Not only does this action get you seen on their page or by their followers, but it also plays on the society of egoists that exists today (especially in the West). Everyone likes to feel valued and important. We have a culture of narcissism (Hey everybody, look at me!). Curators should know the context of our generation and take advantage of this context by curating accordingly. People are looking to be noticed and recognized for their contributions.

4. Craft attention-grabbing headlines.

Some basic psychology. It all comes down to internal instincts: how we seek excitement, drama, gossip, violence, etc. These sorts of headlines also provide stimulation in the context of our hyper-stimulated world. We are always searching for the next exciting thing (and will click once we find it)!

5. Add original input to provide context for readers

Why does this work? Humans love anything new and this method is still quick and easy, so applies to our 'quick and easy society.' It also uses visual data, which is readily absorbed. We still don't want to work to gather this information ourselves ('least work possible' society). Better yet, it is cutting edge and NEW (unlike the other copies on the Internet), which adds flair and also grabs your attention. Original input puts the work in context so that you don't have to.

6. Think like a plastic surgeon

We are a highly visual culture and, as such, we love anything with visual appeal. We will choose something that looks good over what doesn't every time (e.g., think media strategies, marketing, materialism, consumerism, fashion models, the 'ideal' look'). Curators can use graphics to enhance their content, which relates to our visually-based cultural context. We immediately judge value based on how things look over anything else.

7. Borrow someone else's platform

If you only have 55 friends, you may want to post on another platform! Use other platforms to boost your own work. In this society, we do not have a problem allowing others to do things for us. We have everything automated. We also use other people's achievements and fame to further our own. Therefore, platforms are made with this context in mind (i.e., the fact that people may not have the time, resources and skills to build platforms with a ton of followers, so someone else makes the skeleton platform and people fill in the meat with their content). This plan is actually pretty brilliant. Again, this points to the 'quick and easy' cultural modes of today and the 'I have no problem using something someone else made to further my own achievements' culture. Here's a tip: use more than one content format, not just text, visual, etc. Use other formats, such as YouTube! and Slideshare, while keeping in mind that different people use different methods to learn and different mediums to gain knowledge. Remember, the context of the world today is diverse, not everyone gets his or her daily news from the newspaper. We must accommodate the multi-platform nature of the Web by publishing on as many formats as possible to maximize our reach.[85]

8. Create more than one piece of content from each curation effort

In other words, split the content into multiple pieces. For example, one piece of information gathered from the content can lead to a picture shared, a video used and three other texts. This split sets you up to reach additional platforms and share cultural context; it speaks to our desire to 'get the most from the least work/resources used.' If we can have one good story and create five others from it, which will then be shared, we will do that rather than making six original stories.[86]

9. Incorporate a contextually relevant call-to-action

People like to make easy choices and actions, so if you have inspired or motivated them through your content and then include a RELEVANT button or link to another piece of content, they will often click on it. Such a link provides another option for someone to interact with on the site (e.g., a page on environmentalism with a monster list of environmental activists and then a link button at the bottom to a certain organization or charity).[87]

Whatever else you do, contextual relevance is, perhaps, the most important thing you can focus on in your curatorial efforts. As the volume of noise grows, your audience is increasingly counting on you to provide a collection of ideas, elements and voices that are relevant. Context is key to relevance and your audience is counting on you to respect their time and deliver consistent, curated content that helps them to understand the world and discern relevance in, sometimes, not immediately related material. Keeping their trust is critical to your success.

Chapter 12: Monetization and Curation

It wasn't that long ago that curators were thought of as little more than pirates, linking to the work of others and gaining traffic from those links, but as the Web becomes harder to navigate and consumers find themselves looking for smaller, crisper collections of well-curated content, the role of the curator has become accepted as valuable. Now that the pirate label is fading, the question of just how curators should be valued and how revenue should be shared is moving to the center stage.

There are some things that are now accepted in the content creation and Editorial worlds. Curators are important, even essential, in creating coherent content. Curated Web sites are now among the leaders in revenue with sites like *The Huffington Post*, BuzzFeed and Upworthy among the leaders in Web traffic and revenue.

Therefore, the models for monetization are evolving. That being said, there are some models that are emerging now, and they are only going to grow.

Revenue depends on scale, value of the audience to the advertisers and exclusiveness of content. Quality content matters. If you don't have desirable content and an engaged audience, then no monetization strategy will work. Content is

114

still king, curated or created, and it needs to provide value to your visitors.

No matter what type of monetization strategy you embark on, you need to be in direct contact with your visitors. As Scott Scanlon so smartly puts it, you need to own the clicks.[88]

In order for you to use curation as an effective conversion tool for you or your business; however, when it comes to monetizing the curated content, only one thing matters. Once the traffic is on your page, whoever controls the click ultimately determines where that traffic goes.

In the content marketing game, I think this quote from *Business Week* is one of the most important quotes of the last five years: "(t)he smartest people in the world are working hard to come up with ways to get you to click on ads."[89]

Said Scanlon, "Assuming this is true, just think about it...the smartest engineers and scientists at Google, Apple (yes, with SIRI), Facebook, Twitter and Microsoft are spending billions of dollars and massive amounts of brainpower with one goal in mind: To get you to stay engaged and click. I think it is clear what that means in the realm of marketing: Whoever controls the click controls the profit. On the other hand, if you don't control where the click goes, you lose your opportunity to monetize. And that's the name of the game in content marketing. That's why you do it, after all, to monetize. If you are in it with any other motivation, then it's really just a hobby. That's why you must own the platform."

What he's saying is that the platform is where all of the value is created. So, if you're curating on Facebook, Google+, YouTube a page you don't control, then you're unable to control the monetization.

Said Scanlon, "You've worked hard to gain your social capital, but, if you have done so on platforms that you have little or no control over, then everything you've built up is at risk. Also, and perhaps even more critically important, you're ultimately building the value of someone else's assets, while only marginally affecting your own."[90]

So, you need to own the platform and the click. It's that simple. As you gain authority and audience on your platform, you gain control over the monetization.

Monetization today falls into three categories: advertising, subscriptions and ecommerce. Each of these categories can work, depending upon your site's curatorial focus and audience. For some of you, it will be a mix and match of options and revenue sources, so don't be afraid to try different approaches.[91]

Advertising

Advertising used to be something that sites sought to avoid or to do as a last-ditch attempt to find an economic model, but, in recent years, the mantra of 'everything on the Web must be free' has evolved into a more reasonable understanding that something has to pay the bills. Now that curation has emerged as an important and necessary part of the Web, advertising as a way to monetize curated sites has become more expected.

Advertising options for sites include a variety of form factors and choices, among them:

- On Page Display
- Banners
- Links
- Display Advertisements

If you're curating a collection and delivering a consistent audience, then advertising is a reasonable source of revenue. There are a large number of ad networks and each network will provide varying monetization results based on your category, audience, unique visitors and the quality of your pages.

Video pre-rolls

It used to be that only video hosts controlled the value of the on-page content; however, this ownership is now changing with video now driving on-page 'pre' rolls and interstitial video ad units. While this is mostly thought of as a behavior for video pages, increasingly we're seeing video take over ads that run before articles or pages in an interstitial format.

Sponsorships. Sponsorships from advertisers with specific content of interest will drive the highest effective CPMs and the number/coordination of sponsorships is an exercise in optimization. Targeting is tough to do in-house, unless you've got 10M+ users. If you're small, just go through an ad network, and push for a minimum guarantee, if possible. Finally, don't forget that lead gen is a form of advertising (check out how CNET monetizes).

Native Advertising. Native is a new category, but it's fast growing. Native ads are Editorial elements that give advertisers the opportunity to tell their stories in ways relevant to your users. A curated page of content on a subject can often be the ideal environment for a Native ad unit. Just take care to make sure that Native (i.e., sponsored) content is properly labeled or your visitors may become suspicious of the objectivity of your overall curation POV.

Subscription. In categories where a large amount of content exists, sites can offer a curated collection behind a pay wall. What you're charging for isn't the content, which can be found on the Web, but for your unique curatorial expertise and organizational excellence.

Keep in mind that, in order to charge a subscription, you probably need to mix some original 'premium' content with a curated collection. While there is not firm rule about this, a mix of created and curated appears to be the best choice. However, it's a high bar to get consumers to pay for content. *The Wall Street Journal, The New York Times,* Netflix and *The Information* are making subscriptions work on their premium sites. Club sites like Handyman Club, Gardening Club and other niche community sites work when they offer a mix of content, commerce and community for a monthly fee.

Syndication

With syndication, you can license your content to sites with a similar audience and ask for guaranteed cross-links. Don't worry about cannibalization-nothing is truly exclusive in this world and you care much more about brand than anyone else.

Ecommerce. Here's a place where content can drive commerce. If, for example, you have a great site for fly fishing and amazing curated content that includes videos, text,

119

photographs and tweets, then what better place would there be to include links to products that fly fisherman would want to buy? Affiliate links to appropriate commerce sites could provide a solid revenue option for this sort of curated site.

Harsh Agrawal, writing on ShoutMeLoud.com, has some other smart monetization tips.[92] He suggests that if you are curating in a niche topic (e.g., finance, real estate), you can sell your own eBook or use Amazon affiliate and recommend ebooks from Amazon in your category.

As Agrawal explained: "You can also reach out to other experts selling services or products, and tell them about your niche curation-site. The quality of traffic on such niche sites is really high, and the conversion rate would be great. You can use this as a pitching point, and get direct advertisements."

Another way to create value from your curated site is to invite visitors to join your mailing list or subscribe to your site's RSS feed. In both cases, Agrawal correctly pointed out that you are creating tremendous value by building a mailing list. That list can provide you with an appropriate audience for a wide variety of email marketing options down the road.

If you're going to ask for a registration, a pop-up window that invites visitors to register for your daily or weekly newsletter can do the trick. Sites like Mail Chimp can automate this process with an RSS to email system that automatically turns your posts and videos into a nicely-laid-out and automatically- delivered newsletter.

Part 3

Great Curators- Who's Doing It Right?

Chapter 13: What Makes a Great curator: Tips and Tricks

Five traits of successful curators

If you're a curator looking for some boundaries in what feels like the Wild West, here are five best practices to consider.[93]

1. Be Part of the Content Ecosystem

Be part of the content ecosystem, not just a re-packager of it. Often, people think of themselves as either creators or curators as if these two things are mutually exclusive. What a curator really should do is embrace content as both a maker and an organizer. The most successful curators include sites like *The Huffington Post* that embrace the three-legged-stool philosophy

122

of creating some content, inviting visitors to contribute some content, and gathering links and articles from the Web. Created, contributed, and collected — the three 'c's is a strong content mix that has a measurable impact. Why? Because your visitors don't want to hunt around the Web for related material. Once they find a quality, curated collection, they'll stay for related offerings.

2. Follow a Schedule

Audiences expect some regularity, and they'll reward you for it. It doesn't need to be a schedule that you can't keep up with. If you want to curate three new links a day, and write one big post a week, that's a schedule. Make sure to post at the same time each week. This is so readers know when to expect new material from you. Consistency and regularity will also bring you new users, and help you grow a loyal base of members who appreciate your work. A good example of someone who gets why a schedule makes a difference is Jason Hirschhorn via his *MediaReDEF* newsletter. He never misses a publish date.

3. Embrace Multiple Platforms

It used to be that your audience came to you. Not anymore. Today content consumers get their information on the platform of their choosing. That means you should consider posting short bursts on Tumblr, images on Pinterest, video on YouTube, and community conversations on Facebook. And don't leave out established sites and publishers. If your audience hangs out on a blog, you may want to offer that publication some guest posts or even a regular column. Essentially, you have to bring your content contributions to wherever your readers may be.

4. Engage and Participate

Having a voice as a curator means more than creating and curating your own work. Make sure you're giving back by reading others and commenting on their posts. A retweet is one of the easiest ways to help build relationships with fellow bloggers and curators. And your followers will appreciate that you've pointed them to good content. One word here, I never hit a retweet without clicking through to read what I'm recommending. You can also lose followers if you don't put in the effort to recommend material that you really think merits their attention.

5. Share. Don't Steal.

Take the time to give attribution, links back, and credit. The sharing economy works because we're each sharing our audiences, and providing the value of our endorsements. If you pick up someone's work and put it on your blog, or mention a fact without crediting the source, you're not building shared credibility. You're just abusing someone else's effort.

The important thing to realize is that we're increasingly living in a world of information overload. So when people choose to listen to you it's because you're able to separate signal from noise. You provide a clear, contextually relevant voice within the topic or topics that you create and curate.

In the chapters ahead, we'll explore some sites and individuals who are using a list of best practices to build growing businesses and sites using curation. They're different, and they don't all agree on how to curate or which tools or practices to employ - but they're all using curation to build meaningful Internet businesses that are growing.

Chapter 14: BuzzFeed

BuzzFeed is the brainchild of Jonah Peretti, who co-founded the news site *The Huffington Post* http://en.wikipedia.org/wiki/The_Huffington_Post along with Ken Lehrer and Arianna Huffington in 2005. He left *The Huffington Post* in 2011 after it was purchased for $315 million by AOL.[94]

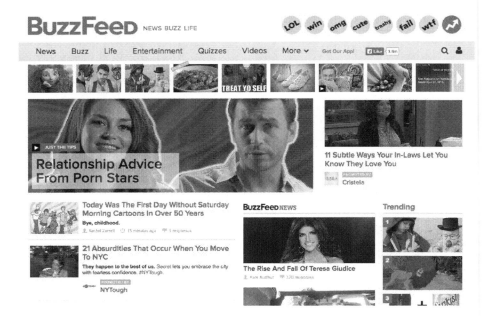

The first time I met Peretti, he was already ensconced in the early phase of BuzzFeed and I was building Magnify.net. The early days of BuzzFeed were driven by discovery of social acceleration. He'd learned a lot at *The Huffington Post* where he innovated testing and optimization of content to drive consumption and sharing. It was his tech that explored *The Huffington Post* headlines in real time, seeing which headlines were working and often A/B testing headlines, pictures and page layouts to improve readership and sharing.[95]

While Huffington was conceived to win the SEO race, Peretti today says that he doesn't care about SEO. He views it as a broken system that optimizes for robots, not humans. "Twitter and Facebook are the front page for content now — people don't go to homepages, content comes to them via social networks. What's exciting to me now is that there are these social platforms like Twitter, reddit, Facebook and StumbleUpon. That means you can create something for humans, not for robots, and still build something massive."[96]

The story begins in 2006 when he founded BuzzFeed, which exploded onto the scene as the next generation of Editorial reporting and infotainment. Described as a social news and entertainment company, the site provides the headlines of the day in current events, culture, politics, entertainment and technology with a hodgepodge of hot topics, special interests and weird tidbits from the Web that are tagged with "LOL, Win, OMG, Fail" and other cyber lingo. The site offers its 150 million monthly visitors the "most shareable breaking news, original reporting and video" content on the Web.[97]

Background

In 1997, Peretti linked up with the John Johnson, head of Eyebeam, a multimedia company based in Chelsea. In search of a Web wizard, Johnson wanted someone to help execute his vision of an online forum for young artists and technologists to share their work.

He came across an email sent by Peretti that went viral containing an exchange that he had with a representative from Nike. The company denied Peretti's request to custom design a pair of sneakers with the word "sweatshop."[98] Soon enough, the email was seen by millions and impressed Johnson as a lightning bolt of attention-seizing content. Peretti was soon flooded with media requests to discuss the controversial topic of labor practices.

Johnson brought Peretti on board with Eyebeam to do research and development. They began by creating and testing viral sites, such as "Crying While Eating," which eventually ballooned into massive visitors who could view people chowing down on their favorite food, while lamenting about whatever was bringing them to tears. Peretti and Johnson soon discovered that they had a viral-worthy product. Based on those results, Peretti was inspired by the idea that led to BuzzFeed's existence: turning these viral appetizers into a main course where this brand of content could be monetized. That vision was realized as BuzzFeed grew into an online conglomeration of news stories, videos, entertainment coverage and the BuzzFeed Community.

Users register and post content, which is then ranked by number of views. There are corresponding award tags that are assigned to those posts that draw the most activity. Posts can range from standalone content, such as a picture with a short description, or lists on every topic under the sun, like "Which Celebrity Would Make the Best President" or "How Much of a 90's Kid Were You?"[99] In 2012, the company hired Ben Smith of Politico as Editor-in-chief. He's been vocal about his vision for the company in regard to it taking a more authentic and serious voice in its journalistic contributions.[100]

BuzzFeed was successful in attracting millions in investment funding early on. Peretti has shared that the company draws its revenue through social advertising where companies can attach their name to "advertorials," - social advertising that's shared and viewed repeatedly by an engaged audience.[101] Essentially, companies can camouflage the hard sell within Native advertising or the packaging of paid-for content.[102]

This reinvention of advertising is using content that's presented as being Editorial to replace the former method of banner and block placements on a Webpage. Some in the industry have cautioned that this new era of advertising blurs the lines between authentic journalism and corporate solicitation.

Peretti says that BuzzFeed's aim is to "work with brands to help them speak the language of the Web."[103] One example can be found in a campaign for General Electric where they created a time machine and users could pick a decade to see what BuzzFeed's content would have looked like based on the timeline. The site also partners with Facebook and Twitter to cycle through sponsored tweets.[104]

A piece by *The New York Times* cites the most recent investment as being of $50 million from Andreessen Horowitz, a venture capital firm in Silicon Valley.[105] In total, most of the company's revenue is generated through BuzzFeed Creative, a team of 75 advertorial thinkers who come up with prepackaged content to be used as a vehicle for brands.[106]

BuzzFeed has rocketed into the stratosphere of social, information-sharing content. Here's a general sketch of the mechanism behind its operation: the homepage is powered by technology that essentially acts as a monitoring device, scanning mainstream sites, such as AOL, *Time*, TMZ and others for viral content. The algorithm is programmed to select pieces of content identified as "viral." That content is then channeled back into rotation on the BuzzFeed site.[107] Slots on the homepage are driven by this viral scanning process as well. The site also uses technology to pick up on individual feeds where certain content might be channeled through the social media streams, eventually surfacing as viral on BuzzFeed.[108]

BuzzFeed's Editorial team examines triggered content and then determines whether that content is assigned a yellow tag (e.g., LOL, OMG, Cute) on the homepage. If the content draws enough clicks, then it earns its own RSS feed.[109] The company's data-science team scrutinizes each piece of content and its origins. They also follow the track it takes via subsequent views to measure its "viralbility."[110]

Editors also come up with new features to test on the site. They then engage feedback about the technology from the users and implement their creative spin on the featured content.

Content is formatted into numbered lists, such as "19 Secrets All Late-Night Eaters Won't Tell You" or "The 7 Deadliest

Selfies" with eye-catching photos and graphics to convey the information. There's also a trending section that lists the top viewed stories on the site.[111]

The quizzes page is a popular feature with visitors and seems to have contributed to a significant increase in traffic to the site - significant enough for analysts to take notice. According to a recent article in *Newsweek*, BuzzFeed records the data accumulated in their quizzes section.[112] Analytics expert Dan Baker commented, "'Most sites record *some* information. BuzzFeed records a whole ton.'"[113] The data is collected by Google Analytics and is a treasure trove of information on Internet users and their preferences and habits.

This collection calls into question the ongoing debate of Internet privacy and how invasive social media tools can be. Christina DiRusso, BuzzFeed's senior communications manager, was careful to point out that the quiz data is collected in bulk and isn't intended to compromise individual privacy.[114]

Social Media

Social Media accounts for 75% of BuzzFeed's referral traffic.[115] The data analytics team surveys how each item of content evolves into viral status from "seed views" into "social views." BuzzFeed measures that data as a "viral lift," meaning how many people discover a trending story on a social site.[116] The company uses social media to connect with their readers, while keeping in step with the pulse of "what's happening right now." It gives readers the opportunity to take part in those conversations. Social media has been and continues to be an integral part of the BuzzFeed operation. It regards Facebook as the "'new front page of the Internet.'"[117]

BuzzFeed makes use of the Twitterverse, interfacing with user activity to cycle through highlighted retweets. Twitter has also been used to collect material for Editorial pieces, one of the most recent being a story by one of its Editors on sexual assault victims.[118]

This mining of the Internet for information and stories that don't have a presence on mainstream outlets is part of what makes BuzzFeed a unique platform for social journalism. Peretti and his team remain focused on how consumption of news is shifting toward social media. The way people get their information has splintered into social-sharing forums and a more individualized brand of news reporting. BuzzFeed has been instrumental in pushing this trend to the next level.

New Directions

BuzzFeed is looking to break new ground in the territory it has already claimed. "'We're organizing ourselves to be a media company for the way people consume media today.'"

Peretti asserted, as quoted in *The New York Times*:

Since Horowitz's $50 million infusion, the company has disclosed plans to introduce new content and technology, and investing additional focus and dollars in BuzzFeed Motion Pictures, the company's Los Angeles-based video production offices.[119] There are also plans to expand globally, setting up offices in Berlin, Mexico City and Mumbai. Their social media agenda will continue to be refined with the development of BuzzFeed Distributed, a team of 20 people whose sole focus will be on content created for social media and messaging apps.[120]

On the journalism side, both Peretti and Smith have expressed their intentions to establish BuzzFeed as a credible news source. Recently, the site removed thousands of old posts that didn't reflect those intentions.[121] The company is attempting to elevate their standards, distancing themselves from the frivolous label of being the site that hosts "click bait" - snappy, superfluous headlines lacking Editorial substance. Part of raising that standard includes their Editor-in-chief

Shani Hilton laying out a policy of explicit standards in their journalistic practices.[122]

As BuzzFeed journeys into its next phase, the founders are keenly aware of the challenges that come with maintaining the company's position as the leader in new social media with growth moving at light-speed. Whatever the challenges and looming competitors, Peretti is confident: "We are building the defining news and entertainment company for the social, mobile age."[123]

"Media and content are human businesses, and it's a problem for humans to give so much power to Google, which is a robot," he told *Pando Daily*.[124]

Takeaways from BuzzFeed:

- Shareability matters in regard to gaining social acceleration

- Facebook and Twitter are the front pages of the Web

- Native ads are where the revenue is today

- BuzzFeed looks at AOL, TMZ and other sites for viral content

- Lists drive sharing today

- Social media accounts for 75% of BuzzFeed's referral traffic

Chapter 15: Upworthy

I f BuzzFeed is the king of curated traffic generation, then Eli Pariser is turning the BuzzFeed model on its head. Pariser is a political organizer turned digital savant. In the days after 9/11, he launched an online campaign to call for a nonmilitary response to the attacks and got 500,000 signatures in 30 days.

Pariser joined MoveOn.org in November 2001. In 2004, he was named the executive director of the company, a position he served in until 2008. Since 2008, he has been the company's board president. As of 2012, MoveOn.org reports a membership of over seven million people. As the Web has become more powerful, Pariser has become concerned about algorithms that provide content to users to meet their personal biases and narrow perspectives.

He coined the phrase 'The Filter Bubble' and wrote a book by the same name that brought these concerns to the forefront of the conversation. Simply put, he noticed that search engines responded differently to questions based on a user's search history. So, someone with a liberal POV would get an entirely different set of responses from someone with a conservative POV. Pariser's history is germane to our topic of curation.

He brings to his work a clearly partisan POV, but, at the same time, is deeply engaged in fostering educated exploration of issues and ideas, looking to illuminate and engage rather than push a one-dimensional propaganda.

In 2012, Pariser launched Upworthy. Upworthy's mission is to host the content at the intersection of the, awesome, meaningful and visual, but, unlike MoveOn, which was powered by email, Upworthy is powered by social networks, in particular Facebook, using the virality of content to promote stories with a liberal perspective on social issues. It has been called "the fastest growing media company in the world." [125] Upworthy's growth challenges some of the assumptions of BuzzFeed, driving content based on meaning and issues rather than mass audience engagement. The numbers don't lie. Upworthy grew to 8.7 million unique monthly views in October 2012 up from six million the month prior.

Upworthy has a team of curators who begin each day reading social media, looking for trending stories. Pariser told *Business Insider*: "We have our team of curators spending all their time looking on the Internet for stuff. We go for visible, sharable stories and really stay away from doing more typical, text-driven articles and blogging. We lean into images and videos."

He also said that not all social networks are created equal. For him and his team, the value of Facebook can't be underestimated. "Honestly, I think [that] part of [our success with it] is [that] we take Facebook much more seriously than many of the other social networks." He continued, "I love Twitter, and Twitter is a fun place to hang out with smart people, but it's a small fraction of our traffic compared to Facebook. The time and attention most sites spend on perfecting their homepages is probably what we spend on Facebook. If you look at our homepage, it's pretty mediocre."

Upworthy isn't a team of content creators, but, rather, of curators, who spend time finding, improving and testing stories to see what catches the attention of their audience. Once they find content that they think has the potential to go viral, the curators write 25 headlines – looking for the words that will catch fire. "The ethos behind the 25 headlines is, you can have the best piece of content and make the best point ever, [b]ut if no one looks at it, the article is a waste. A headline is all about getting the article in front of people," said Pariser. Here Pariser begins to sound a lot like BuzzFeed's Jonah Peretti. Pariser knows that good content doesn't matter if it isn't read or shared. "A good headline can be the difference between 1,000 people and 1,000,000 people reading something."[126]

Pariser is using the same toolbox as Peretti, but with a different underlying motivation. Pariser wants important content to be read and shared and he knows that 'tricking' a reader into clicking on an important video only matters if it then is worth sharing. Otherwise, it's one click and that isn't going to spread.

Upworthy tests tons of headlines for each post and then looks at how many people click on a link once it's been tweeted or liked and how many people share an Upworthy post once they've clicked on it. Then, Upworthy uses the data to optimize its content. So, is Upworthy a content farm or a curation enterprise? Well, they know the answer to that.

In June 2014, the company announced that it spent the past two years building a "culture of curation." Here's how the company told the story on its blog:[127] "What is curation, you ask? It's the process of sifting through the glut of content from across the Web to find compelling, unsurfaced gems with societal importance and delivering them to folks in a way that breaks through the sea of same.

The best curators can find and recognize important things that resonate in a bone-deep way. That's not always easy. The Internet is filled with painstakingly researched white papers on important civic issues. It's also filled with satire, inspiring narratives, thought-provoking analysis, and the things that really engage us at a gut level. The mission for Upworthy has always been to find the middle of that Venn diagram — where the civically important meets the impactful."

Upworthy calls their 'secret sauce' the Iron Man Principle. Again, from their blog, "The idea is to balance creativity and Editorial judgment with technology and data that test assumptions and guide decision-making — one part human, one part machine.

"The key to the Iron Man Principle is to create a culture that uses data in a balanced, heuristic way — not to override human intuition (as data often does), but to guide and challenge it. We want curators to negotiate the data signal with their own Editorial judgment and the review of their peers. This is how you really supercharge impact."

Upworthy thinks deeply about how its curators explore content. "We stress divergent thinking and challenge new curators to look at our site and imagine wildly different realities for it, but with great data comes great responsibility.

We're arming our curators with a window into our audience — a real-time feed of what they're clicking, consuming and sharing. The best curators know that's it not all about them. We want our curators to internalize the feedback, take it to heart, and continually strive to stay attuned to what's resonating. This develops into a powerful instinct over time."

The differences at Upworthy go beyond the Editorial process. As tempting as all that traffic may be, the company is steering clear of conventional advertising. "We're doing sponsored opportunities to sign up - essentially lead gen for causes," Pariser said. "Folks who visit our content pages get an opportunity to sign up to join, say, the Sierra Club. You have to imagine that advertisers will want to get much more interactive," continued Pariser. "We place their messages at the right place, at the right time."

Interestingly, Upworthy's growth isn't particularly translating to views on its homepage. It turns out that Upworthy is bringing its content to the social Web and is perfectly fine with users viewing it there. According to Pariser, "We're not trying to keep people on the site very much. We want them to view the content, share it, subscribe to it, and go on their way. We figure we'll be able to reach back out to them again."

Takeaways from Upworthy:

- Having a powerful voice, POV or bias doesn't diminish the power of curation.

- You don't need to create content to create a voice.

- Recruiting, training and growing curators is critically important.

- Testing various approaches to make content connect with an audience doesn't make your content any more (or less) valuable. It's marketing.

- Using data to illuminate human instincts is valuable.

- Facebook trumps Twitter (at least for Upworthy).

Chapter 16: Waywire

Waywire Networks represents the coming together of a vision and a technology into an integrated platform of quality, human-curated, tech-enabled channels. Waywire Networks is powered by a technology platform that has lead the way in video curation, and resulted in a powerful alignment of video discovery and organization for both enterprise customers and consumers looking for quality curated channels. Waywire was born with a simple mission, make video discoverable and organized. Give publishers a video curation tool and the massive noise around video will find new curated coherence.

For a number of years, the company was known as Magnify.net and supported a growing number of channels. Then, in 2012, Newark Mayor Cory Booker, and co-founders Sarah Ross and Nathan Richardson launched a site with a vision much like Magnify. While Magnify served professional site curators, Booker, Ross and Richardson wanted to put curation in the hands of the millennial generation.[128]

"I've always been very compelled about the democratizing force in social media that is getting more voices engaged in the larger dialogue," Booker told the *Newark Star Ledger*, saying that the site would be a way for millennials "to let their own voices be heard, engage in a different way."[129]

Booker was a believer in curation and was able to share that vision with a growing community of investors and advisors. With industry leaders, including Google's Eric Schmidt and LinkedIn's Jeff Wiener and Reid Hoffman, and media celebrities, like Oprah Winfrey, Waywire has gathered a group of influential believers. By combining enterprise curation and consumer creation, Waywire Networks, a new company with the combined resources, tech and investors was born.

Today, Waywire Networks has two divisions – Enterprise, and Consumer. Waywire Enterprise (enterprise.waywire.com) provides a powerful platform that powers many of the Web's most active and successful video curators. From AARP to TimeOut London to *New York Magazine*, Waywire's video curation tech is driving discovery and relevance for leading sites and publishers.

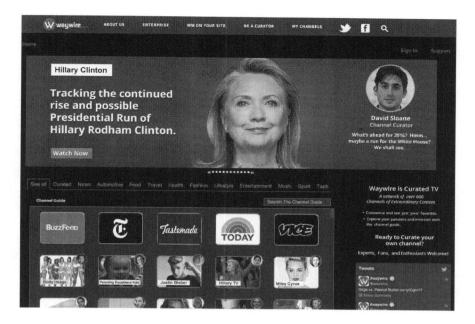

So, how does it work? Well, first, Waywire has proprietary search technology that gives curators extra muscle. A curator working on a site about a particular medical specialty can use key words, tags and programmable searches known as AVDs (Automatic Video Discovery) to explore video sources, including AOL, Yahoo, NBC, Conde Nast, Rightster and CBS. Each of these sources provides high quality video. That video is often delivered with revenue paid directly to the publisher.

Once the AVDs are set up, the curators don't have to search any further. The Waywire technology runs the searches automatically and delivers the results via email directly to the curators' inboxes daily. Using this discovered content, the sites can use a mix of pixel perfect CSS skinned players and

Video Channel pages to provide a mix of on-site videos and video channel experiences. With the shift to mobile that the Web is experiencing, Waywire now delivers HTML5 players and pre-roll inventory that can help publishers monetize their growing mobile audiences.

Since most sites create some video on their own, Waywire provides an integrated video uploader. Once uploaded, the video can be encoded and hosted on the Waywire CDN, which is powered by Akamai, or pushed to a third-party player, such as YouTube!, Vimeo, Brightcove or Ooyala. Either way, hosted video isn't the hard part of video for most sites. It's mixing the created and curated video into a seamless audience experience that gives visitors a deep collection of video to enjoy and share without having to incur the costs of massive video production.

For Waywire Enterprise customers, the ability to search the wide expanse of the Web for video, and use their teams' human intelligence to find and elevate the most relevant content gives them an important leg up in the competitive world of Web video.

On the consumer side, Waywire has partnered with the leaders in their channel categories, providing experts and passionate enthusiasts access to technology that before was only available for thousands of dollars to video curation professionals.

So, as we find ourselves moving toward a video-centric Web, and as the first-screen shifts from the desktop to the mobile device, the ability to trust sites to deliver relevant, contextual video becomes critically important. Waywire believes that technology-enabled human video curation is critical to the growth of niche video channels – and the living room OTT flat screen is not far behind.

Waywire Takeaways:

- For Web video, contextual relevance is key.

- Technology can help, but human curation is critical.

- The nature of narrow-cast gives underserved audiences a voice.

- Curators deserve to get their fair share of the ad revenue.

- No longer can video creators limit how their audiences find their content.

Chapter 17: reddit – Crowd Curation

While most of the curators in this book are individuals, reddit has achieved remarkable popularity with crowdsourced curation. reddit is a phenomenon unto itself. Described by some as a mid-sized country, it was created in 2005 from a Massachusetts apartment by Alexis Ohanian and Steve Huffman. Today, the social network news aggregator has more users than France has people.

The site bills itself as the front page of the Internet. On reddit, users post links to the site, which other users then "upvote," pushing popular posts to the top of the site. I call this a *crowd-sourced curation mechanism.*

It's democracy in media in action and, in the nine years of reddit's existence, the results have been a measure of the

Internet's potential and peril. Today, reddit receives 8.5 million page views per day, as compared to its predecessor Digg, which at its height was getting 238 million unique visitors per year. The important thing to understand about reddit is that it is more than a raw crowdscore, since reddit's algorithm operates a complex system that calculates the "karma" of an individual user. reddit is one of the few sites that allows for both up and down votes, so that stories move both up and down as the crowd responds. Submission time is an important parameter and newer stories will generally rank higher than older stories. The first 10 up votes count as high as the next 100 (e.g., a story that has 10 up votes and a story that has 50 up votes will have similar rankings). Perhaps most interesting is that controversial stories that get similar amounts of up votes and down votes will get a low ranking compared to stories that mainly get upvotes.[130]

reddit's algorithm isn't a secret; in fact, the code base is public and transparent.

Here's how the company describes the operation of the service:[131]

How is a submission's score determined?

A submission's score is simply the number of up votes minus the number of down votes. If five users like the submission and three users don't like it, it will have a score of two. Please note that the vote numbers are not "real" numbers, they have been "fuzzed" to prevent spam bots. Therefore, taking the above example, if five users up-voted the submission and three users down-voted it, then the up vote/down vote numbers may say 23 up votes and 21 down votes, or 12 up votes and 10 down votes. The points score is correct, but the vote totals are "fuzzed."

What is that number next to a username? What is karma?

The number next to a username is the user's karma. It reflects how much good the user has done for the reddit community. The best way to gain karma is to submit links that other people like and vote for, although you won't get karma for self posts.

Why should I try to accumulate karma?

Why should you try to score points in a video game? Why should your favorite sports team try to win the championship? Or, to look at things from a less competitive and more altruistic perspective, read what philosophers have said about the matter - namely, don't set out to accumulate karma; just set out to be a good person and let your karma simply be a reminder of your legacy. Note: reddit makes no guarantees about attaining Nirvana.

reddit Takeaways:[132]

- Encourage your brand advocates to post. reddit focuses on users, not brands, so if you can engage fans of your brand to post, then it will be much better received.

- Do some research to see whether there is already a sub-reddit about your brand or topic.

- Update your news on a calendar. reddit users are looking for the freshest top stories of the day.

- Build a network. If your topic is related to several sub-reddits, consider connecting them to build a network.

- Offer customer service. Customers have come to expect to be able to ask customer service questions on social media.

- Use reddit for marketing insights. If your brand has thick enough skin to take it, you can ask questions on reddit and get brutally honest responses from users.

Chapter 18: Tumblr

Founded by David Karp in 2007, Tumblr is a social blogging site home to 201 million blogs and counting, where users can share current happenings and thoughts along with photos, music, videos and links. The site has templates allowing bloggers to create customized colors, fonts and html.[133] This is an advantage that this site has over its social counterparts, such as Twitter or Google+. Described as "part microblogging, part social networking," the site consistently sees billions of page views and new members in the thousands each day.[134]

Background

A homeschooled kid who taught himself how to write code at the age of 11, Karp was involved in several tech startups before establishing Tumblr, which took him to international hubs like Tokyo and Manhattan, where he now resides. He was the chief technology officer at UrbanBaby, an online forum for moms who divulge their experiences of parenthood in a city environment, specifically Manhattan.[135] When the company was purchased by CNET in 2006, Karp went on to form his own company, Davidville.[136]

In its early days, Tumblr was comprised of a small team, aligned with Karp's visions at the time. Wary of big operations, Karp wanted to try to run his ship with a small team that soon ballooned to over 100 people. Colleagues have described Karp as reclusive, while Karp himself has used the label "antischedule" to describe his working style. Operating on a regimented schedule impedes creativity, according to Karp.[137]

Karp didn't so much invent the format for Tumblr as he evolved it. A German high school student was messing around with a blog template and wanted to create something snappy and shorter, with more links and images and less text. So, Chris Neukirchen created an abridged version called "Tumbleblogs."[138] The site had a solid following and caught the attention of programmers abroad, including Chicago-based techie Marcel Molina.

Molina created a site called Projectionist. In 2007, Molina was contacted by Karp who had seen and was inspired by Projectionist for his project-in-the-works (Tumblr). Over the next year, the two exchanged calls and emails until the communications waned.[139] Karp raised millions and launched Tumblr to the next level. In 2009, Molina moved on to work for Twitter.[140] In May 2013, Yahoo purchased Tumblr for 1.1 billion dollars, which stirred up controversy within the Tumblr community, especially among its avid users. They feared that the acquisition would flood the site with corporate advertising and other Yahoo-initiated tactics. Marissa Mayer, the CEO of Yahoo, made official statements to the contrary via her own Tumblr page, assuring users that Tumblr would not be adulterated by the Yahoo brand.[141]

Functionality

Tumblr, in its very basic form, offers a venue for people who actively create new content and want to present it in blog format; it's also for people who stream curated content that they want to share with those individuals who have similar interests. [142] Setting up an account is a straight-forward process that entails providing one's email and creating a username and password. From there, users can choose their blogging palette and upload content. There's a default Tumblr theme and a whole range of original designs, one of the unique features of Tumblr that can be used with the premium membership. The dashboard in the right column controls customization, settings, drafting and saving posts and uploading other media.

The site can be explored to find content that's tagged with categories, such as music, politics and humor. There's a spotlight feature that posts highlighted or popular blogs within a certain category. The site also has a bookmarklet that can be added to the Web browser for items on the net that users want to migrate to their Tumblr page. Favorite posts within the Tumblr community can be saved in one place on the dashboard. Bloggers can recycle or re-post other content from their favorites. Users can also connect with their friends through the site's friend finder, a list of those individuals using Tumblr.[143]

Tumblr and Social Media

Although it trails behind Facebook and Twitter, Tumblr continues to expand its territory and scored a platinum endorsement from Apple in March 2014 when the company publically embraced the site, creating the isee5c.tumblr.com[144] A study conducted by Simply Measured, a social media measurement company based in Seattle, found 31 of the top 100 brands use Tumblr.[145] Companies like Disney, MTV and Ralph Lauren use Tumblr to connect with their customer base. Adidas was the first to use Tumblr to launch a major ad campaign.[146] Demographically, 13- to 25-year-olds use Tumblr more than Facebook.[147] It's also ranked in the top 20 sites in the US and saw a growth of 74% in 2013 versus 40% for Twitter and LinkedIn in the same year.[148] In 2013, the site released an upgrade to its iOS app with a social media sharing feature embedding Twitter and Facebook in the application. Users now have an enhanced social sharing usability as Tumblr has been savvy about incorporating social media streams into its service.[149]

Tumblr is an international network with several countries around the globe using the service. Its content is streamed in 13 languages. As of January 2014, the top five countries active on Tumblr were the US, India, UK, Brazil and France.[150] Seoul has been on record as having the most unique visitors and 66% of its overall visitors were below age 35.[151] Visitors spend an average of 14 minutes on Tumblr, more than Twitter and Facebook.[152] Although the site is popular with the younger demographic, marketing experts advise business owners of the benefits of Tumblr as the users can quickly disseminate information about brand as demonstrated with larger corporations like Coca Cola and MasterCard.

As for Tumblr's future, Karp wants to sharpen his brand by finding new horizons of creativity. In an interview with Forbes in 2013, he said, "The way that we want to make it better is that we want it to be this perfect platform for creativity; we want to empower creators all over the world, following in this legacy of technology companies like Adobe and Apple, two of my favorite companies growing up, that would actually let people make stuff that they couldn't make otherwise, right? That's an amazing, amazing thing."[153]

Four Ideas for How Brands Can Use Tumblr

Thea Neal, posting on *ignite social media,* provided a great breakdown of the best ways that brands can use Tumblr.[154]

Post Frequently

Many brands have joined Tumblr, but don't frequently update. We see this issue with hair brand Frederic Fekkai's Tumblr, which has only been updated five times since November 2012. Most of their updates are long interviews with stylists and aren't ideal for reblogging on the platform. However, brands like Adidas and Sprite blog photos and gifs, without extensive text, multiple times a day.

Be Succinct

Tumblr isn't the place for long-windedness. The most popular reblogs are photos or gifs. Tumblr is fueled by the reblog, which works just like a retweet. However, on Tumblr, it's still acceptable for a blog to consist solely of recycled content. If you want your brand to be noticed, then strong visuals are your best bet.

Pull From Pop Culture

If your legal department lets you post pop culture memes or gifs, then do it. Online shoe store Solestruck is a favorite among Tumblr users, with its posts getting hundreds of reblogs and likes. The brand posts things that are relevant to its crowd, not just relevant to its products.

Watch Your Audience

More than 65% of Tumblr users are under 35 and the site continues to be one of the most loved by teens. If your brand doesn't resonate with this age range, then Tumblr might not be the place to occupy. Pixar manages to appeal to a wide range of ages with funny gifs, real photos and original sketches from its films.

Tumblr Takeaways:

- Make your content "tweet worthy"
- Use your content to 'help' not 'hype' your readers
- Follow, like, reblog[155]
- Post frequently
- Be succinct
- Pull from pop culture
- Watch your audience

Chapter 19: Pinterest

This chapter starts with a story. A number of years ago, my friend Brian Cohen, now the chairman of the venture group New York Angels, called me. "Steve...," he said. "I've got a guy you've got to meet. He's smart, he's ambitious and he's got an idea that is totally in your wheel house – curation." I always trust Brian, so I was happy to take the meeting. A few days later, Ben Silbermann was sitting across the conference room table showing me a demonstration of his product, which was then called Tote...like a tote bag for collected content. At that point, Ben was looking for angel investors. I had done a few investments, but I wasn't sure that people wanted to curate images, so, I passed. That, as they say, wasn't such a good decision.

Today, Silbermann's Pinterest is on fire – a massive success and I remain a fan and a friend, even if I didn't pony up when I should have. That's the great thing about entrepreneurs, they see the future in a way that others can't.

How Does Pinterest Work?

Pinterest is a social bookmarking site where people "pin" their hobbies and interests in collage format: everything from cooking to pets, entertainment, decorating tips, travel, music, crafts and sports...any topic of interest and all its derivations presented in eye-catching graphics on a personalized pinboard.[156] Pinterest functions as a virtual storage house of cherry-picked content from the Internet that people want to favorite and share. Users can connect to other boards and "re-pin" content from people with shared interests.

Background

CEO Ben Silbermann founded Pinterest in December 2009 and launched the site in March of the following year. Inspired by "Pirates of the Silicon Valley," Silbermann discarded plans to attend medical school and moved west from his home state of Iowa.[157] He worked for Google in customer support, analyzed data and worked in product design. Silbermann had a desire to develop his own products, but hit a wall with Google as it didn't extend him the opportunity. He quit soon after.[158] Venturing out on his own, he tried to raise money with little success until he hooked up with his college friend Paul Sciarra in New York, the future cofounder of Pinterest.[159] After a period of trial and error, Silbermann scored a deal and Pinterest was born.

Silbermann later connected with programmer Evan Sharp (third cofounder), who designed the Pinterest layout.[160] The site began as an invitation-only network of 5,000 users, many of whom were from Des Moines and each of whom Silbermann reached out to personally to gauge their response during the site's beta phase. The user-base jumped to 10,000 in its 9th month of going live. In 2010, Victoria Smith, who created the "Pin It Forward" program, came on board as a community manager, implementing the concept of trading virtual pins.[161] In March 2011, an iPhone app was created, catapulting the site's user-base. By August of the same year, *Time* had placed Pinterest on its list of "50 Best Sites of 2011."[162] By 2012, Experian Hitwise reported the site's official status as the third largest network in the country.[163] In August 2012, Pinterest dropped its invitation-only criteria and pulled in a $100 million dollar investment from a Japanese company. With over 70 million current users, as of 2013, the site has secured over a half-billion in investment revenue.[164]

Pinterest A-Z

When examining the practice of curating content from the Internet, Pinterest is a perfect example. Pinboards are an amalgamation of images, links and videos filtered from the Web to create a "social currency" or valued content that others want to access and share. Infographics deliver the tangibility of this social currency and Pinterest acts as the virtual exchange. Setting up an account is quick and easy. An email, Facebook or Twitter account is used to activate a new account. Facebook and Twitter are automatically synched with Pinterest. Account settings can control what information originating from Pinterest appears on other social media sites.[165]

Once an account is established, a user can create a personalized pinboard. As with Facebook, a profile photo and personal stats are posted on the main page. Friends can be found via the Facebook interlink, and users can invite friends or follow existing users.[166] The "Pin It" button is downloaded into the taskbar as a tool to pin items that are found on the Web to the board. Clicking on each pin takes you back to the item's originating site. Content within the Pinterest community can be "repinned" from other boards, and friends can pin on each other's boards. Community boards can be created as well.[167] Multiple boards can be created under one account to categorize interests. As such, users can select which boards they want to follow of other users who have more than one board, which keeps with the practice of curating.[168]

For the business-savvy, adding a Pinterest account to a company's marketing arsenal is a common recommendation among social media experts. Experts also provide such tips as: careful selection of a profile picture that's "Pinterest worthy," creating a profile that succinctly defines the business and connecting with similar ventures on Pinterest.[169] Small business consultant Ryan Pinkham suggests creating three boards: one for products and services, a second that's customer-oriented and provides a place for Q&A engagement and a third that's straight-up creative, giving customers a blended taste of professional services and personal interests.[170] Outlined strategies exist for repinning in order to boost visibility of one's business. Repinned content from other boards can potentially connect a business with new customers, particularly from boards that have a large following. Curating value-added content yields attention, allowing an opportunity to connect with new customers, especially if that content resonates with the business' mission. Taking into consideration how many times the content had been previously pinned is part of the strategic formula.[171] *Forbes* contributor Jayson DeMers, anointed Pinterest "one of the best and most popular image-based platforms around."[172]

Pinterest has also found its way into the classroom as teachers and professors are incorporating it into teaching methods. Colleges, such as Texas State and Colorado State University, are using the site as a way to create out-of-the-box assignments for students. One of the pioneers is Andrew Lih at the University of Southern California who made use of the site for his entrepreneurial class in the early days before its massive popularity. Lih gave his students instruction to gather art clips and other visuals that captured certain themes, an assignment that wouldn't have been as effective using conventional means.[173]

The fundamental benefit of Pinterest is that it adds uniqueness to Web presence. It can draw active interest and raise visibility for an individual or business. As pointed out in a post on Gigaom, we live in a world where so many things are homogenized. As such, Pinterest is a great tool to use to stand out.[174]

Stats and Social Media

Pinterest is predominantly used by women (they make up 80% of its user-base). Of those women, 84% are still active four years after joining.[175] A recent report by *Marketing Land* states that 92% of pins are made by women - a significant stat given that women tend to be the decision-makers with household spending. In the age-demographic category, 18- to 29-year-olds make up 27% of the users and 30- to 49-years-old make up 24% of the users. Race and ethnicity is evenly spread with Hispanics tracking at 18%, just below the average of 21% across all other ethnic groups.[176] Data reported in 2012 showed that 70% of the user-base used Pinterest for shopping ideas.[177] Also, the peak time for sharing on Pinterest is at night.[178]

Pinterest interfaces with Facebook and Twitter and is set up with an option to create an account by signing up through those sites. When signing in from Facebook or Twitter, it auto-tags content to identify posts that originated from Pinterest. As of 2013, Pinterest was the fastest growing social media site.[179] In the same year, it emerged as the leading social media site for ecommerce, garnering 41% of the customer traffic of all the social networking sites. [180] Compared to other social media sites, Pinterest is more effective in driving traffic and generates more referral traffic than Google, YouTube!, LinkedIn and reddit combined.[181]

One of the newest features added to the site is "Place Pins," a function where people can pin their favorite geographical destinations, guides or locations anywhere on the map. Jon

Parise, who helped program Place Pins, underscored its built-in value as Pinterest is a multi-cultural, international network. He also pointed to the four million existing Place Boards on Pinterest to show that the new feature was the next logical step.[182] This added functionality helps businesses be located much faster by their customer base.

Pinterest has been estimated as having a valuation of $2.5 billion, although Silbermann has been quoted as saying, "We don't make any money" and continues to be restrained in making any grand projections for the future. He has shared thoughts about coming up with creative ways to improve the site and cater to users and their lifestyles. "When we think about this mission - we think there's a direct link between the things people think, the things people do, and the things people buy."[183]

Brands Who Are Curating Pinterest Boards

Sarah Powell has a great overview of big-name brands on her blog. Here's her quick tour:[184]

The Cooking Channel

The Cooking Channel has plenty of boards dedicated to all kinds of different recipes, holidays and food types. There are some fun and creative boards here, too, including one called "Play with Your Food List" and "A World of Hot Wings."

Whole Foods Market

Of course, there's the obvious – recipes, food items, holiday cooking. The not-so-obvious and really interesting boards here are: food art, kitchen gadgets and a whole board dedicated to reused/recycled DIY projects.

Pottery Barn Kids

The company's boards are broken out in a variety of ways, including the obvious nursery and kids' room decorations, but, beyond that, you can view boards with pins for kids' parties, recipes, arts and crafts projects, and baby shower ideas.

National Guard

The National Guard boards focus on families and the work that the National Guard is doing here and around the world.

Humane Society of New York

Naturally, there are boards featuring the pets that need to be adopted. What's even more compelling are the boards of happily adopted pets, a board dedicated to the needs of the organization and fun boards featuring pet photography and cool pet abodes.

The Weather Channel

Besides the boards called "Winter" and "Spring," there's a board dedicated to cold weather gear, weather gadgets, teaching the weather and funny weather.

Kelly Lieberman has been compiling a list of the brands on Pinterest (using a Pinterest board, naturally). Her list can be found at: http://www.pinterest.com/kellylieberman/brands-on-pinterest.

Pinterest Takeaways

- Curation of images means more than just posting your content and images around your brand.

- It's about sharing images and videos that are important to your customers' lives and passions.

- Pins should be curated from all types of places, not just the brand's own site.

Chapter 20: Brain Pickings. Maria Popova

Maria Popova is a curator 100% of the time. At the ripe old age of 30, her blog, "Brain Pickings," is widely read and often the source of links on-sites that count on her curation savvy. She described Brain Pickings as "your LEGO treasure chest, full of pieces across art, design, science, technology, philosophy, history, politics, psychology, sociology, ecology, anthropology, you-name-itology."

To curate the site, Popova reads hundreds of sites a day, posts to her blog and Tweets thoughts of the day on her Twitter handle: @brainpicker. *The New York Times* described her curation mix as an "exhaustively assembled grab bag of scientific curiosities, forgotten photographs, snippets of old love letters and mash notes to creativity — imagine the high-mindedness of a TED talk mixed with the pop sensibility of P. T. Barnum — spans a blog (500,000 visitors a month), newsletter (150,000 subscribers) and Twitter feed (263,000 followers)."

The New York Times listed among her fans and followers "an eclectic group of devotees, including the novelist William Gibson, singer Josh Groban, comedian Drew Carey, neuroscientist David Eagleman, actress Mia Farrow and Twitter founders Biz Stone and Evan Williams."[185]

She told *Lifehacker* that she spends 450 hours a month curating for Brain Pickings, which is to say, her exploration and curatorial revelations don't come out of some magic technology, it's actual hard work.

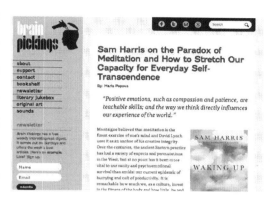

She's put together her own system, which she describes this way: "I live and die by Evernote. As a notorious note-taker, marginalian and quote-collector, I save between 10 and 100 snippets of text a day from articles that I'm reading. Everything is meticulously tagged and organized, so I can search and cite it later in articles and talks. I've also recently switched to Pocket for all my time-shifted reading needs. It's exquisite, very visual, and much more conducive to making materials organized and manageable than Instapaper, which I used to use. Then, of course, Google Reader is a staple. I'd say at least two thirds of my Web reading is done via RSS."

She's got a regime, a ritual you might call it: blogging three times a day and scheduling 50 tweets a day. Music is also programed as part of her ritual. "I have various music modalities for different purposes—for reading books, mostly classical, lots of Vivaldi; for light reading, *All Songs Considered*, KEXP's *Song of the Day*; for writing longer pieces, lots of jazz; and many, many more," she told *The New York Times*.

Like many of her peers who are a first generation of content curators, she sees herself as a modern day librarian of sorts. She sees her function as both Editorial and organizational, comparing herself to a Dewey Decimal System for the Web.

As a curator, Popova has fans. Paola Antonelli, a senior curator at the Museum of Modern Art, says a good curator is someone whose own taste has somehow become the taste of millions. "What Maria has is the DNA of millions of people," Antonelli told *The New York Times*. "She somehow tunes in to what would make other people dream, or inspire them in a way that is quite unique."

Popova says she views her job as "helping people become interested in things they didn't know they were interested in, until they are."

"She's a celebrator," Princeton professor and former State Department official Anne-Marie Slaughter said. "You feel the tremendous amount of pleasure she takes in finding these things and sharing them. It's like walking into the Museum of Modern Art and having somebody give you a customized, guided tour."

Popova's work reminds me of a great series of interviews with authors in *The Paris Review*. Edward Tuffe, the Yale professor emeritus of computer science, statistics and political science, told *The New York Times*. "I read those over and over for inspiration, but also to try to understand the meaning of a creative life."[186]

Clearly Popova wants to be part of that tradition. "I want to build a new framework for what information matters. So much of what the Web is presenting lowers people down. What Paris Hilton ate for breakfast. By contrast, the vast majority of its gems remain untapped."

So where is the line between promoting the good work of others and simply lifting it? "As custody of content becomes more tenuous, there's a risk that we may end up passing around and putting topspin on fewer and fewer original works, which has created a growing sense of unease among both digital immigrants and natives that the end of "ownership" could eventually diminish the Web's value."[187]

Popova so strongly believes in the importance and future role of curators that she's taken a leading role in trying to codify a code of conduct for Web curators. Called *The curators Code* - http://www.curatorscode.org - Popova and her collaborators are working to set 'rules of the road' for curation.

On her blog, she explained the need for a framework for curation: "As both a consumer and curator of information, I spend a great deal of time thinking about the architecture of knowledge. Over the past year, I've grown increasingly concerned about a fundamental disconnect in the 'information economy.' In an age of information overload, information discovery — the service of bringing to the public's attention that which is interesting, meaningful, important and otherwise worthy of our time and thought — is a form of creative and intellectual labor, and one of increasing importance and urgency. A form of authorship, if you will. Yet, we don't have a standardized system for honoring discovery the way we honor other forms of authorship and other modalities of creative and intellectual investment, from literary citations to Creative Commons image rights."[188]

Brooke Gladstone of NPR's *On The Media* explained the code this way: "Maria Popova, of the site brainpickings.org, along with Tina Roth Eisenberg, aka swissmiss, have created what they call *The curators Code*, Unicode icons that you can embed in a blog post or article that's a shorthand for attribution. A sideways S icon is a 'via,' V-I-A, which attributes and links to the original material. A looping arrow icon represents a 'hat tip,' which will take the reader to where you first encountered the content that you're sharing. *The curators Code* serves as a kind of breadcrumb trail that allows the reader to trace both the source and inspiration for an article."[189]

Today, Brain Pickings generates the bulk of her income, but there are no ads on the site. Instead, she solicits donations and earns an affiliate fee from the books she recommends on Amazon. Said Popova: "The secret, of these and of any life skill, I believe, is practice and stubbornness." Two great attributes for curators to have.

Brain Pickings Takeaways

- Read more than you write – a lot more

- Evernote is a powerful tool for curators to use to organize their efforts.

- Music can help create rhythm and focus.

- Curators like Popova understand they're building a new Editorial tradition.

Chapter 21: Birchbox

B irchbox is an online beauty and skin care supplier from which members can have sample products delivered to their door in a specialty box. The New York-based company was launched in 2010 and has seen steady growth. Birchbox represents the alternative method that consumers use in their search for products. Subscribers to the site fill out a profile with information about their product preferences, skin type, sensitivities and current products that they're interested in trying.

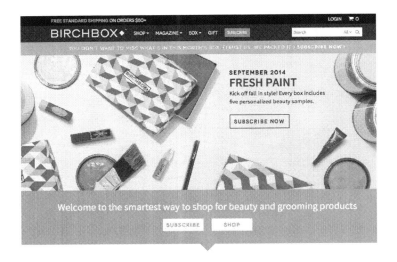

Based on a subscriber's profile, Birchbox sends him or her an assortment of samples, custom-picked for his or her needs, including skin care, fragrances and makeup. The boxes are priced at $10 for women and $20 for men.[190] Subscribers can then order full-sized products and submit follow-up feedback and suggestions on the Birchbox site to fellow subscribers. The site also features content to guide members on how to use certain products.[191] There's a points system where members can earn points through purchases, referrals, surveys and feedback on the samples that they've tried.[192] Subscribers can shop on the site for items in categories such as hair, fragrance, home and food products, makeup, skincare and other specialty items, such as tea accessories. There's also a *Birchbox Magazine* with tips and trends in the beauty and skin care industry.

Birchbox is one of several online entities that combine highly-personalized customer service with the convenience of "one click" shopping. Katrina Lake, the CEO of Stitch Fix, was inspired to create her online fashion company to help the busy woman save time with assembling and updating her wardrobe. Like Birchbox, customers fill out a profile that allows the company to pre-select items that best fit their tastes, lifestyles and body types, creating a "new shopping experience."[193] This shared mission, to offer an alternative and unique shopping experience, is what the brand is built on. "We use curation and personalization," asserts Katia Beauchamp, founder of Birchbox.[194] So far, customers have responded well to the formula. With this crop of growing companies like Birchbox and Stitch Fix, the prospects are enormous for tech entrepreneurs as ecommerce is projected to be $1.5 trillion of global market sales as of 2014.[195]

In order for the model to succeed, customer feedback needs to be a key component for a company like Birchbox and its viability. Engaged subscribers discussing their individual experiences with products fosters attention, paving the way for new customers. Consumers trust other consumers when exploring new products. This old-school, word-of-mouth tactic is driven by the rewards system that Birchbox has in place, giving their subscribers an incentive to contribute feedback.

With technology added to the equation, word-of-mouth spreads far more quickly. On the retail side, the company is supplied with hundreds of brands, many of which are well-known names in the industry, like DKNY and Cartier. Featured on its homepage are products with the highest number of reviews and current best sellers.

The site also lists product ratings with the corresponding number of stars as ranked by the users. How these users are linked to the products is a result of carful research performed by Birchbox's data science team. Data mining is used to analyze customer preferences and needs and where they're spending their time searching for certain products, which helps the company determine the contents of each box for a particular customer.[196] Boxes are shipped out by the 10th of the month with shipment notifications emailed to subscribers. Each box is assigned a tracking number. Birchbox has 800,000 subscribers and 50% are active shoppers on the site. A quarter of the company's revenue is from its site sales. The company recently secured a $60 million investment to expand its market.[197]

Birchbox and Social Media

As with any ecommerce venture, Birchbox employs social media streams to execute its products and attract interest. Keeping pace with how consumers find their information, a social media presence is vital and allows creative outlets for promotion. For example, to promote its "Birchbox Man" department, the company shared advice and tips geared toward men on Facebook and Twitter. It also developed a special Facebook quiz series.[198] In addition, the company rolled out instructional videos on YouTube!. In 2012, the company hosted Twitter parties on Monday nights, looking to stimulate conversations not only about their products, but also beauty/lifestyle interests in general.[199] The site also has a Tumblr page with blog posts that cover tips, celebrity features and snack recipes. The Pinterest page is a collage of beauty, inspirations, favorite Birchbox products and seasonal promotions. In addition to social media, the site offers video chats with members of the Birchbox team as well as mobile app downloads and Instagram snapshots.

Birchbox Horizons

Although ecommerce is a continuously evolving and profitable business strategy, online companies are seeking ways to establish themselves in traditional environments (i.e., brick-and-mortar stores). With larger competitors, like Wal-Mart or Macy's, online specialty companies see the bigger picture of having a presence both online and offline. Statistically, ecommerce has a narrow slice of the market in total retail sales.[200] Companies are taking their personalized appeal and transferring it into the real world with in-person, specialized customer service. Andy Katz-Mayfield, the co-chief executive of Harry's, the online retailer of men's high-end shaving products, summed it up with his perspective: "'It's about creating another channel to sell [a] product.'"[201] The company recently raised funds to set up a store in New York. Others partner with existing stores, such as Nordstrom, where the online retailer, BaubleBar, stocks and sells its merchandise.[202]

In July of 2014, Birchbox opened its flagship store in Soho, New York. The two-story open space showcases hundreds of products with an appealing layout for the browsing shopper. Customers can schedule appointments with in-house makeup artists and beauty experts for one-on-one guidance.[203]

Taking it several steps further, the store uses cameras and heat sensors to track which products customers gravitate toward. iPads are part of the in-store operation through which customers can access a "Product Matchmaker" program that offers measured analyses of which products are best-suited for their style and needs.[204]

The company also plans to include WiFi analytics in order to collect consumer data, such as frequency of visits and product purchases.[205] Ultimately, the company wants customers to walk away with the Birchbox experience, taking the mundane out of shopping.

Other companies are looking to get into the Birchbox game. It's estimated that there are over 500 existing specialty box companies competing for subscribers. [206] Experts in the industry have identified the potential pitfalls of the model. Liz Cadman of *My Subscription Addiction* has outlined important items to be mindful of during the curating process. Curating a target demographic might not cast a wide enough net and may alienate customers who aren't represented in the data, yet whose interests and spending behaviors are equally relevant. Presentation is everything. Cadman emphasized the added touch of including a small card or letter that details why each item was selected, making that personal connection with the customer backed-up by an effective customer support team, which is integral to the success of an online operation.[207]

In 2012, Birchbox acquired its Paris-based competitor JolieBox. The company then expanded into international territories with availability in France, Spain and the U.K.[208]

Birchbox Takeaways

- Understanding your reader or customer makes custom curation more valuable

- The line between ecommerce and content is blurring

- Encourage and embrace customer feedback

- Use social media to generate new customers and speak to your base

- Different social media sites provide different opportunities to communicate and connect

Chapter 22: 20SecondStory

Olga A. Levitsky's career was spent in sales support functions with large enterprise technology firms, helping sales organizations demonstrate the value of the company's products to potential clients. However, this is harder than it sounds. According to Levitsky, "there are many different products and solutions to position, and many types of clients in different industries and at different levels of scale and maturity. There was a persistent problem of the corporate marketing organization or the product management team wanting to tell one story, and the sales professionals wanting to tell a different one." Over time, she realized that the tools and processes that helped enable effective storytelling in an enterprise context were relevant to businesses of every size and set out to start her own company to provide that service. Her reasoning was simple: "What large companies like the ones I worked with previously have, that mid-sized businesses lack, are organizations that curate and manage internal knowledge – most smaller firms are running at full speed without the infrastructure to gather and analyze the stories they are creating every day through their interactions with customers and partners. I saw an opportunity to provide this type of curation and analysis as a service to customers without the capacity to handle it internally, as well as to teach large firms how to do it more efficiently."[209]

Today, she's turned her process into a business. She calls it the 20secondstory.com. She explained her process, as it relates to curation, to me. "Companies are already telling stories to their customers, partners and communities every day, through the quality of their work, their customer service and support, and their branding. The marketing department may think it has a handle on these stories, but a quick trip to the customer support department or a day of shadowing the sales team will often reveal huge gaps between the 'official' story and the one that is actually being articulated to the marketplace." She continued, "Getting a handle on an organization's 'real' story is a first step – we get a hold of that by analyzing the volume of content that customers generate every day in their regular interactions, whether transcripts of support calls or copies of sales collateral or social media content. Looking at this content collectively allows us to break down the authentic, lived story of an organization into its 'building blocks,' basic elements that recur when personnel are put on the spot to tell their company's story in day-to-day business interactions."

With these building blocks, she says that organizations can refine the story and align the organization around it. Instead of a firehose of competing internal messages, she helps companies get down to a simple set of core concepts that can be taught and communicated by individuals of any level of expertise, in any organizational role. According to Levitsky, "Once the organization has fully understood and embraced its story, and transformed its operations to reflect that story, we take it to a broader audience. The most successful brands are the ones where customers themselves do most of the selling, by communicating the story of the brand in the way they use and share the products. These types of advocacy can be enabled with targeted, consistent communication of the essential building blocks of a company's story."

As a way to explain her service, Levitsky shared the story of one of her clients, a winery called Russian River Vineyards. Russian River Vineyards went through a significant brand transformation. For a number of years, it had a small, but stable business selling good wine from local vineyards to local customers. It knew that it had the ability to take its product to the next level, so it invested and increased quality at every level: brought in French oak barrels, improved the production and bottling processes, and hired a new and very respected winemaker.

The result was that the quality of the product shot up – the company started winning awards, scoring 90+ points, etc. The problem was that the company's costs also went up and, consequently, so did the price of the wine. So, the company called Levitsky. "They had a gap between the story they were telling with their product and the story that their long-time customers understood about the winery. Customers who had bought from them for years were showing up to find 20%, 50%, even 100% mark-ups on the bottles. So, even though the product was much better, they were losing customers."

20secondstory needed to curate the story and retell it to customers. "When we analyzed their communications to customers and their products, we saw that, in many ways, they hadn't brought their customers into the story. They had been making these changes in the background, but not improving the customer experience of the winery, and not communicating the nature of the transformation. We helped them improve the face they presented to customers, and worked with them to find a few essential narrative threads to communicate to long-time customers to make them feel like part of the journey. The physical location and experience of the winery was changed, the branding on the bottles improved and the visibility of the winemaker and other key players in the business increased, so that customers could see the new talent at work. At the same time, we introduced their story to new venues to attract higher-end customers from the broader region and visitors to the area that would be interested in the story of the evolution of this local winery into a serious contender in the market for premium wines." The results were a total success. "Over time, we saw the traditional customer base return with a greater willingness to pay the higher prices, and new customers flood in."

Why is it critically important to curate the story you tell customers? As Levitsky sees it, it is because the nature of the world we're marketing in is changing and changing meaningfully. "One of the trends we've observed (and that contributes to the name of our firm) is that the time each person is able to focus is getting shorter because more content is competing for a limited supply of attention."

It's not just happening with customers; your team is facing the same overwhelming flood of information. "Your personnel are bombarded with competing messages from their colleagues, customers, peers at other firms and, often, even getting mixed messages from you as the boss. Content is created across the organization, but people consume content in the context of their specific role and responsibilities," said Levitsky. "Curating what they see and hear down to what is essential to their own jobs, and making it consistent and authentic with the goals of the organization as a whole, is a huge challenge as business content increases in volume and velocity."

20SecondStory

Takeaways

- Curators like Levitsky add value and deserve to be paid.

- Companies need to tell their stories well, consistently and clearly.

- Use building blocks to build your story.

- Don't be afraid to ask for help.

- Content is created across the organization, not just for PR or community relations.

Part 4

Tools and Techniques

Chapter 23: Curation Types and Styles

Rohit Bhargava was one of the early thinkers on curation, having written a blog post that remains prescient to this day. The Manifesto for The Content curator [210] wrote, "A content curator is someone who continually finds, groups, organizes and shares the best and most relevant content on a specific issue online. The most important component of this job is the word 'continually.' In the real time world of the Internet, this is critical."

The 5 Models of Content curation

Over time, the idea of content curation has felt increasingly like a catchphrase that is really encompassing many smaller activities that are adding structure and insight to the cacophony of information being published online. What if we could define not just content curation as a macro activity, but look at how curation might be applied in very specific situations? Here are five potential models for content curation as a starting point for an exploration of the field.

Aggregation

A flood of information exists online and Google can only give you a best guess at the most relevant results for your search, even though there are millions and millions of pages returned for any search result. Aggregation is the act of curating the most relevant information about a particular topic into a single location. It often takes the form of catalog-style blog posts that list "27 Great Resources for Small Business" (or similar aggregations). Volume is not typically an issue when it comes to aggregation, so, in this case, you still may have hundreds of pieces of source material, but, just the fact that it is in a single location and not in several different places, has a high value for people interested in a particular topic.

Distillation

The idea behind distillation is that adding a layer of simplicity is one of the most valuable activities that someone can undertake. Distillation is the act of curating information into a simpler format, where only the most important or relevant ideas are shared. As a result, quite a bit of additional content may be lost for the sake of simplicity; however the value comes from the fact that anyone digesting this content no longer has to contend with a high volume of content and can, instead, consume a more focused view of the information.

Elevation

The smaller ideas that are often shared online in 140 character bursts or pithy mobile phone images may point to a larger societal trend or shift. Elevation refers to curation with a mission of identifying a larger trend or insight from smaller daily musings posted online. Encompassing much of what many trend-focused sites do, this can be one of the hardest forms of content curation because it requires more expertise and analytical ability on the part of the person or organization during the curating. The benefit is that it can also be the most powerful in terms of sharing new ideas.

Mashup

This term is often used in the context of music to describe the growing trend of taking two or more pieces of music and fusing them, but there is a wider implication for mashups in relation to information. Mashups are unique curated juxtapositions where a new POV is created by merging existing content. Taking multiple points-of-view on a particular issue and sharing them in a single location is one example of this type of behavior and describes the sort of activity that takes place every day on Wikipedia. More broadly, mashups can offer a way of creating something new, while still using content curation as its basis because you are building on existing content.

Chronology

One of the most interesting ways of looking at the evolution of information is over time, especially how concepts or our understanding of topics has changed over time. Creating a chronology is a form of curation that brings together historical information organized based on time to show an evolving understanding of a particular topic. It is most useful when it comes to topics where understanding has shifted over time as it can be a powerful way of retelling history through informational artifacts to prove how experiences and understandings have changed.[211]

Chapter 24: YouTube. Video Host or Video Curator?

YouTube has a big problem. It simply has too much video. Up to 2011, YouTube was a massive stew of how-to videos, squirrels on skateboards and some wildly popular, but relatively underground self-made video entrepreneurs. What wasn't widely reported was that the volume of video being uploaded to YouTube was growing tremendously. In June 2007, users were uploading six hours of video every minute. Then, two years later, it was 15 hours every minute. By 2012, it had grown to 72 hours of video per minute, representing a more than tenfold increase in the past five years. Today, more video is uploaded to YouTube in a day than all three major US networks have broadcast in the last three years. This amount has turned out to be both a blessing and a curse. YouTube is the world's largest repository of video, but finding a video in that massive content collection has become remarkably difficult.

So, quietly, YouTube has embarked on a mission to evolve beyond its history of clips and clicks into a full-fledged channel. Actually, a channel of channels. To make this change, it made one big public bet and launched a super-secret project at the same time.

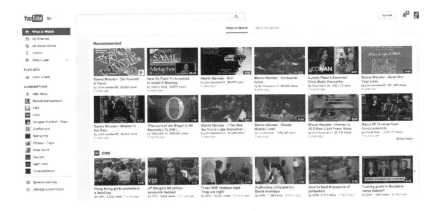

The World Before YouTube

It's easy to forget that there was a world before YouTube. A world where video was hard to find, hard to share and impossible to publish, unless, of course, you were a huge television studio. But, happily, those days are long gone.

Today, rarely a day goes by when a political candidate isn't dealing with the fallout of a YouTube gaffe or a foreign government isn't blaming YouTube for some sort of insult or injury.

You'd hardly know YouTube is at the center of a firestorm when you enter the large, airy lobby in San Bruno. Sure, the front door is locked – presumably security after the worldwide protests from the *Innocence of Muslims* film trailer – but, other than that, it's serene. The photos of founders Chad Hurley and Steve Chen are prominently featured in the lobby. Humming through the building are an army of video reviewers, engineers and project managers happy to continue to foster the growth of a service that is roiling governments, movie studios, publishers and Madison Avenue.

The new video royalty is a growing community of "YouTubers" who are creating videos that connect with a new Web-connected video audience. Simply put, this former headquarters of The GAP is now ground zero for the future of what used to be known as television.

Two YouTubes Emerge

The new YouTube is, in many ways, the new Hollywood. 'YouTube Originals' is now a $300 million bet, partnering with the best-known content creators, celebrities and YouTube channel stars to fund and produce video channels. Now, a year later, the first 100 channels have been launched from partners including *The Onion*, Bonnaroo, NewsCorp's Wigs Channel and *Motor Trend*. The top 20 of these big sexy Channels are drawing over a million views a week.

The channels that are succeeding are, however, not particularly highbrow as they feature scantily clad women, hot cars, music and cartoons. Much like cable TV itself, it is mass audience fare with a special focus on young men.

However, YouTube has also been secretly looking down the road to a world of millions of clips in high quality collections of deep, rich content. To manage it all, YouTube is quickly evolving from a creator to a curator of content. Which is why Dror Shimshowitz is spending all of his waking hours trying to figure out how to attract a whole new type of user to YouTube. Shimshowitz leads a team of product managers, building out YouTube's curation roadmap. As he explains it, curation has the potential to be the secret sauce for YouTube 2.0. "YouTube used to be all about uploading content, but now, going forward, [for] a YouTube channel, you'll have a hard time discerning content that was uploaded by the channel and content that was curated from other sources. At the end of the day, I don't think the viewer really cares."

How will YouTube go from an upload center to the engine that powers the video-curated Web? For that, Shimshowitz looked to today's TV formats for a clue. What he found may surprise you. "If you think about TV shows like ESPN's *Sportscenter*, that's essentially what these formats are. Clip shows. They have some hosts, talk for a few minutes and then they go to some content that they didn't create, but are pulling from other sources. Now, we're making that format available on YouTube. Anyone can use the giant library of video content and start to create these hosted programs."

YouTube wants to turn audience members into creators of curated TV programs about sports, music and entertainment. In fact, YouTube has discovered that makers of content aren't necessarily the best curators of content. Makers tend to gather up their own content, while pure curators will explore the wide expanses of YouTube and curate content. Just what does this new breed of YouTube curator look like? Maybe someone like you.

Shiva Rajaraman is a first-generation American, born in Chennai, India. The product of UC Berkley and Wharton, a lover of both stories and technology, he found himself inexorably drawn to the world-changing power and impact of YouTube. Today, with a warm smile and crisp eye for details, he is the director of product management at YouTube. "My dad, who's in his mid-60s, he grew up in this tiny town in India, almost like a village.

He hadn't been there for 10 years and he was about to go back. My mom had been sick, so they hadn't been able to travel. He just wanted to see how things had changed," explained Rajaraman. "Someone had posted a number of YouTube videos. They'd walked through his old town, year after year, and there'd been all this change. Each one of those videos had maybe 10 views, but he found them on YouTube and ha[d] this whole flashback to his early days and start[ed] sharing them with everyone he [knew]. Every social network he use[d]. He sign[ed] up [for] social networks just to share these videos. That was the moment I was like 'this actually has an impact on people in small places and plays a role in documenting history.'" It was also the moment that his Dad became a curator of videos about Thiruvarur on YouTube.

So, it seems like a curated YouTube is on the way and the reason is pretty interesting. Web video is moving from the desktop to the flatscreen and the TV viewer has a very different expectation of how video behaves. "If you think about what you do when you come home at the end of the day and turn on the TV, you don't go searching for programs," says Shimshowitz. "You pull up your DVR – where you have 10 to 20 shows recorded and put one of them on. Or you go to your favorite station where you already know it's channel 264 or your bookmarked channels on your set top box. That's how easy we want YouTube to work."

Curation is a meaningful shift for the YouTube team, having spent the past seven years making the site the world's biggest repository of video content. However, with the living room flatscreen TV on the horizon, there's a 'curate or be curated' wind blowing at YouTube. "A curator is the best one to tell a 'meme' story because all that content comes from hundreds, if not thousands, of creators," says Rajaraman of videos like the

Rebecca Black meme. That, right now, is an element of YouTube that we're focused on."

As Web video shifts to the living room, viewers watching programs or channels, is much better than clips. "Having users curate content in channels is one of the best ways to get people watching more YouTube on TV," said Rajaraman.

Already with the channelization project just beginning at YouTube, the numbers are massive. YouTube reports more than 1 billion views a month as of September 2014.[212]

The average viewer spent 282.7 minutes, or more than 4 1/2 hours, watching YouTube videos during the month. YouTube views could be on the site proper or on one of the hundreds of thousands of sites that embed YouTube players. In the world, it hardly matters. As Shimshowitz explained, "Our business model is the same no matter where the video is played. Our perspective on YouTube is we want to be on as many video screens around the world as possible."

What accounts for the growth? It turns out that it's not one single thing. First, the company increased video lengths, then raised file size limits, but, most importantly, the growth of mobile phones and tablets as both content creation and consumption devices have driven usage through the roof. The result is what Shimshowitz modestly called "the first truly global video network in the world" and he's right.

Of YouTube's 800M monthly viewers, 70% are from outside of the US and a stunning quarter of all views are from mobile devices. Just to put all those numbers in perspective, in 2011, YouTube had more than one trillion views. That's almost 140 views for every person on Earth. As Chris Anderson, the curator of the TED conferences, wrote recently: "Video has the ability to accelerate knowledge. And already YouTube has changed the world in ways large and small. It's turned faraway places into digital neighbors. It's given us to tools to share personal stories. It's helped shine a bright light on bullies and gay-bashers. It's given individual educators, like Sal Khan, the platform to build an educational community. Almost everywhere you look, in the arts, science, politics, justice, music and entertainment, the modest video Web sharing site that Chad Hurley and Steve Chen began in 2005 has shaped how we tell stories, and how we see and hear each other."

Now, YouTube is embracing the next phase of video. It's called curation. A uniquely human activity that brings together often diverse things, creates new experiences and makes content contextual. Curators are sometimes creators, but often not. The skills are related, but different. If YouTube gets it right, then the job of video curator could truly be a whole new job that turns the noisy YouTube video firehose into an elegant and accessible video gallery, one built and organized just for you.

YouTube's curation Vision - The Impact

Now that YouTube has revealed that curation is core to its strategy for contextualizing video content and that curators will be paid, leaders in the Fair Use and Remix community are taking notice.

Pat Aufderheide is acknowledged as one of the country's leading experts in fair use and a passionate advocate in the field. She heads the Fair Use and Free Speech research project in the Center for Social Media within the School of Communications at American University. She has been a Fulbright and John Simon Guggenheim fellow and has served as a juror at the Sundance Film Festival, among others.

According to Aufderheide, curators deserve this new-found place in the content ecosystem. "I think curators are in the same class of creative actors as Editors and museum/gallery curators. They know a field of production, they exercise standards, they use that knowledge and judgment to showcase work in new contexts that add meaning." Her book, co-authored with Peter Jaszi, *Reclaiming Fair Use: How to*

Put Balance Back in Copyright, is a powerful voice for advocacy. "I think all culture always has been a Remix Culture. The illusion that creators are wholly original in their creations is just that, an illusion. I believe that curators create new material–the collection that they create by selection. This is the most participatory and productive era of cultural expression in the history of the world."[213]

How does YouTube's decision to compensate curators impact her world of remixed and re-imagined video? "It is encouraging to see signs of monetizing the work of curation," said Aufderheide. "Monetization will reward higher levels of effort in curation and articulation of Editorial standards. I do not mean that this field of activity needs policing; I mean that there is a very loose notion, at the moment, of what is involved, and as the activity is elaborated, ways of valuing it will emerge; monetization will be a useful spur."

Just how important is it to share, remix and create new works from existing media? "The emergent economy has shareability built into it. At the same time, this is and has been a bedeviling moment to be an incumbent media company, especially with bricks/mortar issues–towers, antennas, printing presses, etc." However, challenges to existing business models notwithstanding, Aufderheide said that we're at an exciting and critical crossroads. "Limiting that shareability means crippling one's participation in [the new] economy."

Of course, it's the early days and while YouTube's decision is an important step forward, no doubt the balance between sharing and protecting content will raise complex new issues. "As monetization of spreadable culture grows, more and more people will become actively interested in their own monopoly rights under copyright. At the same time, that they will need their fair use rights to create work. So, creators need to know both sides of the copyright balance because most of us want and need both sides of it," said Aufderheide.

Google, Relevance and Video

Ever wonder how big Web video has become? Well, Comscore's numbers show that 186.9 million Americans watched online content videos in the month of June 2014. Google ranked #1 with 153,328 billion viewers.

A very long time ago, in what now appears a distant memory, there was a promise of a world where information would be available, easily accessed, shared and organized. Google did a remarkable thing. It built a search engine that could find what you were looking for magically and deliver it to you seamlessly. It was – and is – a wonder of the modern world. While in its early days, Google wasn't an AdTech company, it found out quickly that organizing the world's information created a tremendous opportunity for advertising. As such, Google AdWords was born in October 2000. The original idea came from Bill Gross at Idealab and was named GoTo.com, later renamed Overture. In October 2000, Google launched AdWords with a simple sentence on the homepage: "Have a credit card and 5 minutes? Get your ad on Google today."

Unlike Overture, Google made two brilliant innovations. Overture's auction model let advertisers buy their way to the top of the listings, a simple auction where the highest bid got the most exposure. However, in a pay-per-click world, Google realized that this approach would fail since irrelevant ads would pollute the pages and bad ads meant no clicks. Instead, Google invented a 'clickthrough rate' to measure an ad's relevance. Google incorporated user behavior into the equation and so an ad with a lower bid, but more relevance, would rank higher. The result was the new "economy of relevance," as noted author and entrepreneur John Battell famously explained it.

That economy turned Google into a massive business and changed the way that advertisers used the Web. Today, AdWords is Google's main revenue source, generating $42.5 billion in 2012. So, all is good in the world of Google.

Along the way, however, the Web changed. People formerly known as "The Viewers" or "The Audience," emerged as both consumers of content and CREATORS of content. Today, we blog, tweet, check in, share, retweet and link and all of that sharing looks to an algorithm like a never-ending expansion in content. At the same time, brands, media companies, business publications, magazine publishers, book publishers, data aggregators and research firms were jumping in to the content creation arena. Most puzzling for both advertisers and Google was that they were all making video.

Google is smack in the middle of this puzzle and has been testing several ways to turn noisy video content into relevant, ad-worthy inventory. So far, there have been a few of false starts and few big wins.

Then YouTube was handed over to Susan Wojcicki. Wojcicki was employee #16 at Google and the company literally was started in her parent's garage. Wojcicki developed AdSense, which many would say funded the growth of the Web by allowing sites, large and small, to get paid by showing Google ads on their pages. Little known fact: Wojcicki has been deep in video for a long time. As early as 2006, she was running Google Video, which was set up to compete with YouTube. Instead, she argued in front of the Google Board to buy

YouTube for $1.65 billion. Shortly thereafter, Google purchased YouTube and Google Video was shut down.

Google's challenge in video advertising has two major threads. Users of AdWords represent a new community of advertisers. The low cost, ease-of-use and simple measurable results created a massive new user-base of relatively small dollar advertisers. Anyone with a credit card and a keyboard could be up and running with contextually relevant ads that generated clicks and sales. It was a magical elixir. However, video ads haven't behaved in the same way. Google has shared a variety of tools to make the creation of video ads user-friendly, but they haven't seemed to connect with the same early-adopter advertisers that launched AdWords into the stratosphere.

Advertisers who might have supported 'long tail' content have been slow to shift to Google's self-serve model. Long tail was a concept conceived by Chris Anderson, and written about in *Wired* Magazine in October of 2004.[214] As YouTube's traffic has grown, along with Google's continued interest in the increasingly important Web video ad market, it makes sense to meet the market need with YouTube "select," an offering of quality 'brand-safe' channels. Which isn't to say that YouTube isn't a darn big business, it is. A serious $5.6 billion dollar business in 2013, up 65% over 2012, which can be, at least in part, attributed to the growth of YouTube on mobile, with small screens making up 40% of its traffic now, compared to 25% last year. Google said on an earnings call in 2013 that it's a remarkable jump as just 6% of YouTube traffic was mobile in 2011.

So far, the innovation and revenue has happened on YouTube's most popular and highly viewed channels. Yes, PewDiePie is generating significant revenue, but he's also driving a stunning 5.4 billion views. Monetization has been growing for channels on YouTube that deliver audiences that look and feel like cable TV. These channels have large audiences and broad topics. However, the revolution that began with AdSense, fueling remarkable growth for Web sites and blogs, has, so far, eluded Web video. This statement isn't a criticism of YouTube; far from it. It has created the platform for video discovery, but moving video revenue to niche video content may be less susceptible to a centralized sales approach.

The puzzle is this: if YouTube's niche audience lives in their embedded network, with contextually relevant video appearing on pages that provide context, community and appropriate and related content, then that's where the revenue and sales are likely to come from. What percentage of YouTube's more than 153 billion viewers are watching video on-sites other than YouTube.com? That data isn't public, but sources say that it may be as much as 60% of total views. Turning that audience into revenue would be a huge business for Google and a powerful new force in revenue for content creators and curators working in the niche network economy.

No one knows this better than YouTube's new CEO Susan Wojcicki, who's been pretty vocal about how important the channelization of Web video is going to be. "There will be some device that brings a lot more Internet to the TV, to the living room. At that point, I'm pretty confident that TV will look a lot more like online video," Wojcicki told *Forbes*' Robert Hof. "People will have all these different channels, they'll be able to choose what they want to watch, everything will be on-demand. I think all the different existing players will adapt to that environment."

So stay tuned. As Web video continues to evolve, so will revenue for programming. Finding the path forward for channelized niche content on embedded sites can't be far behind.

Chapter 25: Curation with Text Tools

Text is the center of the curation universe. Why? Because it's far and away the most prevalent form of communication on the Web and its sheer volume makes curation a critically important solution to separate signal from noise.

There is no shortage of text-based curation tools, and they're constantly evolving. What follows is a journey into some of the best-known tools and solutions for text curation, though it's by no means exhaustive. There are new solutions coming on line every day.

1. Scoop.it

Launched to the public in November 2011, Scoop.it hit the ground running, snagging more than 75 million visitors during its first 18 months.[215] With Scoop.it, everyone can be a smart and powerful publisher.  The tool allows you to discover information that's pertinent to your business or area of interest, grab it, add your thoughts and then publish it to your blog or social networks. Its social networking function, appealing look and vast research capabilities are just a few of the reasons why Scoop.it has become the content curation tool of choice for many brands, students, educators and organizations.[216]

Guillaume Decugis is the Scoop.it CEO and cofounder. His previous business, Musiwave, was a pioneer of mobile music back in the early 2000s, introducing many of the first hit products in that market. He grew it into the leader of its space, powering the music platforms of major mobile operators worldwide, before Microsoft eventually acquired it in 2007. After graduating from Polytechnique in France, Decugis earned a master's degree from Stanford University in 1995.

Marc Rougier is the president and cofounder of Goojet and Scoop.it. Prior to this position, he was the president of Meiosys, a startup in the virtualization space that was acquired by IBM in 2005.

So what makes Scoop.it stand out from its competitors? The San Francisco-based company butters its breads with the belief that it takes more than algorithms to organize the

Internet's content in a smart and meaningful way and believes that the marriage of big data semantic technology and human curation is the best solution for helping brands efficiently and effectively publish relevant content.

Mission of the Software

In an interview with VentureBeat.com, founder Guillaume Decugis summed up the company's vision: "A growing number of people, professionals, businesses and brands have to publish online to develop their visibility, reputation and brand. This is time-consuming, and it is hard to produce relevant quality content to rise above the noise. We help them find content that relates to their areas of expertise, so they can feed their sites, social media channels, search engines and newsletters."

Decugis and his team wanted to give curators more dominion over published content and they wanted to do it in a way that's seamlessly integrated into their workflow. "We became obsessed with how to discover content. Information overload is a problem and we have a big vision to organize the Web, starting with helping people to publish better, more meaningfully, and in a more rewarding way."[217]

How It's Used

Scoop.it allows you to create a simple webpage for a single topic. Educators who teach about a specific topic (a holiday, country, person, etc.) in depth can aggregate articles on the subject matter on one page.

Bloggers can publish magazines for colleagues or like-minded types on topics they think are interesting or pertinent topics.

Educators can use it to organize, in one location, materials that might be used across different classes. A Scoop.it page can be used to aggregate educational videos, online quizzes, spelling resources and other similar items.

Examples of Use - Real World Examples

A college professor[218] from Canada's George Brown College used Scoop.it to curate information on the past, present and future implications of consumerism for our society.

The Law Offices of Bornstein & Bornstein and Bay Property Group in San Francisco work in tandem to assist local property owners, landlords, commercial clients and multi-family investors by offering property management services. Their Scoop.it page[219] is dedicated to that mission.

Doug Peterson is a computer science instructor at the University of Windsor in Ontario, Canada. He has a Scoop.it page devoted to Groundhog Day. [220] I know what you're thinking: "I wonder if *Groundhog Day* and Bill Murray made the cut?" Yes, they did! He also curates a page on QR codes.[221]

Scoop.it info and Takeaways

- Scoop.it makes publishing easy and makes its users seem like real experts in their areas of interest, which was the founders' goal.

- It presents a clean, sleek look. It's relatively simple to use and requires sophisticated algorithms as well as human creativity to perform effectively.

- Scoop.it is free to join and provides basic capabilities. Premium services are available starting at $12.99/month.

- The upgraded version provides increased topic and social sharing limits, customization and analytics.

- Scoop.it is an offshoot of Goojet, which, according to Crunchbase.com, was the "first mobile social media dedicated to Web content discovery."[222]

- Educators, students and brands have embraced the app.

2. Curata

Founded in 2007, Curata is Web-based business-grade content curation software that allows companies to build rich content by seamlessly discovering, refining, organizing and analyzing relevant information and then distributing it to their target audiences.

Pawan Deshpande is the founder and CEO of the company. As such, he is responsible for the company's vision, management and advanced development initiatives. Deshpande has held software engineering positions at Microsoft and Google and was awarded patents in social networking and natural language processing areas. He earned his S.B. and M.Eng. in Computer Science from the Massachusetts Institute of Technology.

Why Marketers Use It

Speed + Efficiency: <u>One4Marketing.nl</u> claims that content curation takes 20 minutes or less per day using Curata.[223]

Intelligent Organizing: The software recognizes oft-mentioned and trending topics in your content. Based on your history, it <u>automatically organizes</u>[224] and categorizes your content using a classification system. It also enriches your content with related pictures, quotes and videos to keep your target audience engaged.

Seamless Sharing: It integrates with many popular third-party platforms, such as Wordpress, HubSpot, Marketo, Drupal, Twitter, Google+, LinkedIn and Facebook.

All-in-One Functionality: In addition to producing remarkable in-house content, Curata enables you to find, grab and organize information published on different platforms and re-distribute that information on multiple platforms, including email.

Mission of the Software

In an interview with Curata founder Pawan Deshpande explained his impetus for starting Curata and how the focus evolved: "When I started Curata, the idea was to empower users to pull together content on any topic they were interested in and share [it] with a larger audience. I realized two things along the way. First, marketers were hungry for fresh, relevant content. The second [was] that there [was] a need to selectively 'curate' the content, not simply pull it together. We quickly evolved our product to serve these needs and become a tool focused on content curation and launched it as Curata. The rest is history."[225]

Brands use Curata to increase visibility, keep customers engaged and attract new customers.

Examples of Use - Real World Examples[226]

The Oregon Wine Board is a semi-independent Oregon state agency managing marketing, research and education initiatives that support and advance the Oregon wine and wine grape industry. The organization used Curata as a way to regularly engage with local wineries and industry professionals. In an interview with Content Marketing Institute, the Oregon Wine Board director, Charles Humble, said that curating a newsletter[227] using Curata has been easy: "Since launching our Oregon Wine Newsroom, we are regularly syndicated by Google as a trusted news source. We have a small staff and this is something we could never have accomplished without curation. Our members are thrilled with the results."[228]

IBM developed its Big Data & Analytics hub to be a dynamic and credible source of information from across the web for its prospects and clients. Realizing the importance of curated content to complement its own created content, IBM turned to Curata's content marketing software to find, organize, annotate and share information from across the web. "Curata software is the principal way the site is infused with content that is balanced for visitors to educate themselves," explained Matt Carter, program director, IBM Digital Marketing, Big Data & Analytics.

The company is headquartered in Boston, Massachusetts.

In May 2014, Curata received the MITX award for the Most Innovative B2B Technology.[229]

Curata was founded in 2007, two years before the terms content marketing and content curation were coined.

Curata info and Takeaways

- Curata is a trailblazer in content marketing.

- Curata is not for the casual content curator.

- Curata offers three business plans: Basic ($349/month OR $4,188/year); Professional ($667/month OR $8,004/year); Enterprise ($999/month OR $11,988/year).

- There is also a special 'agency' pricing provided upon request.

- Curata is suited for business users who want and need a deeper content curation experience.

3. List.ly

Creating a top-ten or best-of list has been simplified by List.ly. The tool enables bloggers and brands to curate, crowdsource and engage readers via live embedded list content inside blog posts.

According to List.ly cofounder Shyam Subramanyan, 30% of all Web content are lists or contain list content.[230] Founding partner Nick Kellet contends that, in most normal blog posts, bloggers have to identify and write about each list item, so, as soon as the list is published, it becomes stale. List.ly squashes that problem by allowing users to create lists, embed them in their blogs and then let their community of readers continue to do live updates, which allows the list to stay fresh and relevant.

In addition to co-founding List.ly, Nick Kellet has created companies in the B2B and the B2C domains. He is as inspired by the challenge of creating new categories as curating old ones.

In the business intelligence space, he created a visual segmentation tool called Set Analyzer, building on the work of Reverend Venn and George Boole, proving that you can curate old ideas to form new ones. As people still struggle with the complexities of Boolean logic, pairing it with the visual Venn diagram created a much simpler way to display data selection and segmentation. Business Objects acquired Set Analyzer, now called SAP.

In the board game space, he created and self-published GiftTRAP, which has been translated into 12 languages. GiftTRAP gamifies the act of gift-exchange. GiftTRAP has won 20+ awards globally, including a Spiel des Jahres award, the board game equivalent of an Oscar.

List.ly isn't cofounder Shyam Subramanyan's first startup. He also co-founded bHive Software, Inc. in 2007 and served as its CEO until 2010. Subramanyan has 10 years of entrepreneurial experience.

Previously, he was one of the founders of Mentorware before which he was building AI and data mining solutions for the Bank of America. Subramanyan earned his undergraduate degree in Computer Science from the University of Madras in India and a master's degree in Computer Science from the University of Florida.

Mission of the Software

List.ly's main mission is to make embedding lists into blog posts efficient and easy. So, what's the big deal about lists? Kellet explained: "From the time we're born and our name is chosen from a list of baby names, to the time we die and we're checking items off our bucket list, we're obsessed with lists. When it comes to business, it's no different. We will read other people's lists regarding our business and industry, partly just to prove how smart we are. We'll scan their list and note that we already knew each item, and come away feeling great about ourselves. Or, we'll find a point or two that we didn't know and come away thinking that we're now even smarter for having educated ourselves on that point."[231]

How It's Used

A history teacher can use List.ly to create a list to around a specific topic to engage students and spark collaboration. For example, a teacher could use a list of "The 10 Most Significant Inventions in History."

A brand could create a list of ideas for future products and allow their customers to weigh in.

A writer could create a list of ideas for future book topics and allow readers to chime in

Examples of Use - Real World Examples

Marie Ennis-O'Connor is a social media consultant and speaker. She is also the author of *Beyond the Buzz: Healthcare Social Media*. Her List.ly page is dedicated to healthcare. Specifically, she has copious lists that provide the best resources and support for those suffering from chronic and terminal illnesses. On July 30, 2014, her list of patient support communities on Twitter[232] appeared on List.ly's 'Trending List of People' page.

Doug Kessler is the creative director and cofounder of Velocity, a B2B marketing agency. According to his List.ly profile, he tweets about B2B copywriting, social media and tech marketing. He has a list on content marketing tools,[233] of course.

Scott Scanlon is the CEO of You Brand, a digital marketing company. He, apparently, is a lover of books. He has many different lists on many different book topics. I love to read, too, so Scanlon's <u>Best History Books</u>[234] list gets a nod from me.

List.ly info and Takeaways

- Including lists in digital content isn't a new phenomenon, but most lists are static and unchangeable. List.ly sought to change that.

- List.ly is free to start.

- List.ly offers two premium services, one for the blogger or content marketing professional and the other for brands with multiple team members who moderate collaboratively.

- Both plans are $9.99/month or $99/year.

- If you're a blogger or brand whose business can benefit from creating blog posts embedded with live, collaborative and updateable lists, then List.ly is the right tool for you.

4. Storify

When a major news story breaks, it takes milliseconds to appear on multiple social media feeds across the globe. Instantly, the Internet is flooded with eyewitness accounts, photos and opinions. Storify enables users to collect bits of information about a particular topic or event from various social media platforms, such as YouTube, Instagram, Twitter and Facebook, and then take those bits to create their own stories. It's a tool that many major news outlets and organizations use.

Cofounder and CEO Xavier Damman moved from Belgium in the summer of 2009 with the vision that there are voices on social media that deserve to be published on mainstream media. This vision was the foundation of Storify.

He founded Tribal in 1999, a site that gathered student content from around Belgium and was published in a 30,000 subscription magazine distributed nationwide to high schools. He built content partnerships with leading brands, such as Microsoft. Damman earned a master's degree with distinction in Computer Science from Belgium's Leuven University.

Cofounder, specializing in business development, partnerships and publisher relations, Burt Herman is also the founder of Hacks/Hackers, a worldwide organization bringing together journalists and technologists. He previously reported for The Associated Press (AP) during a 12-year career, heading the AP's office in Korea and founding a bureau that covers the five countries of the former Soviet Central Asia. Among other assignments worldwide, he was an embedded reporter with the US Marines in the Iraq war, covered Afghanistan after Sept. 11, traveled several times to reclusive North Korea and covered the Asian tsunami and Pakistan's nuclear program.

Herman was a Knight Journalism Fellow at Stanford University, a program for distinguished journalists selected for a year of study. He also received his B.A. with honors in Political Science and M.A. in Russian and East European Studies at Stanford University.

Storify is headquartered in San Francisco. It was acquired by Livefyre in 2013.

Mission of the Software

Storify's founders recognized that most people desire to be informed, but often lack the time required to sift through hordes of information to get to the facts. "People are busy and just want the story," said Storify cofounder and CEO Xavier Damman during an interview with *Joyent*. "Our goal is to enable our users to make sense of what people are reporting on social networks."[235]

How It's Used

Organize Social Media Responses to an Event

Storify can be used to build a post based on people's reactions to certain events. For example, when Google released Penguin, there was a storm of content on Twitter and Facebook.

Another approach is to use Storify to cover the history of a particular subject. So, instead of curating content that involves pulling current responses, users can pull social media content, videos, images and documents that relates to the *history* of the event.

A different approach might be to create a post that is based on a single topic.

- Storify works nicely for pulling together a conversation that may have happened over a period of days, weeks or months.

- Storify, as its name implies, is also great for creating a narrative that can help your readers makes sense of an event.

Examples of Use - Real World Examples

In 2012, Facebook's IPO was big news and market forecasters and tech gurus alike wanted to know how the offering would impact the industry. Storify user Mike Cassidy brilliantly grabbed bits from Lockepick, Twitter and Facebook to explain what the Facebook $38 IPO really meant for everyone.[236] The post was smart, engaging and funny.

Democrats wanted to extend the payroll tax cut back in 2011, which would have saved the average American family $40 per paycheck. Opponents dismissed it, saying that $40 wasn't a lot of money. So, the White House took to social media to find out just how far $40 could stretch.[237]

South Africa and the global community celebrated Mandela Day on July 18. The United Nations used Storify to see how the world committed itself to #67minutes of service.[238]

Storify info and Takeaways

- Storify allows users to effortlessly curate text, documents, videos and images to tell stories using social media.

- It's a favorite tool among journalists and non-media bloggers. It makes its users seem smart, reliable and, sometimes, witty.

- Storify has a free version and a premium service for media organizations, publishers and other individuals who require an enhanced experience.

- Twenty-two of the top 25 media outlets use Storify as well as the United Nations and the White House.

5. Bundlr

Bundlr enables users to select the most relevant information about a particular topic of interest – be it photos, videos, tweets, presentations or articles – and then create "bundles" that can be shared. It may seem a lot like Storify, but, according to founders Filipe Batista and Sérgio Santos, Bundlr is the answer to Internet clutter. "We're afoot with an information overload. New sources and mediums are emerging and each specialist is finding his way through all being published online. But we're lacking the tools to quickly select the best we find on the Web, organize and share it.

"With Bundlr you can create bundles of any kind of content: articles, photos, videos, tweets and links. Cover real-time breaking news from your sources. Wrap up an event with a collection of online feedback. Build a page where you pick the most relevant content on your area of expertise.

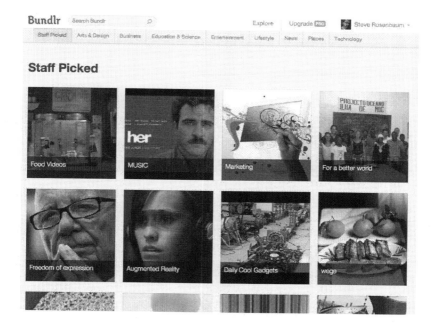

"Using [the] Bundlr browser button 'Bundle This,' you can clip content while you browse the Internet. Just press the button to save the content you want, and the meta-data around it, to the bundle you pick. Each bundle will have its own public webpage you can share freely. In later features, you'll be able to filter clips, create visualizations and embed bundles on any site."239

The real-time updates, collaboration features and ability to embed pages is what the founders believe sets them apart from competitors. Here's what makes it different in the founders' own words: "First, our tool guesses beforehand what the user wants in a webpage. In a YouTube page, it's obvious that the user wants the video, [while] at Flickr, [it's] the main image. Second, we do not only clip the image but all the metadata surrounding that image. For instance, publishing date, geolocation data, author, views, etc. This is true for every site we support. If a webpage is supported, it means it was tailor-made to work with Bundlr so that the clipping process will be as seamless as it gets. Third, we don't limit the layout inside the timeline format. We show the clips in a grid. In the future, with all that metadata we collected, we can get very creative with clip layouts.[240]

Filipe Batista and Sérgio Santos co-founded the company and met during college at the University of Coimbra while studying computer science. A developer and entrepreneur, Santos completed his education at the University of Coimbra receiving a Masters in Computer Science. Batista elected not complete his undergraduate studies. Prior to starting Bundlr, he was the COO at JeKnowledge, the Junior Enterprise of the Faculty of Science and Technology of University of Coimbra.

Mission of the Software

Bundlr's mission is to help Internet users "skim through all of the noise"[241] to select relevant multimedia content and share it with their networks.

How It's Used

Content curators can use the app to create 'bundles of links' surrounding many topics.

Examples of Use – Real World Examples

- On May 27, 2011, news:rewired hosted a one-day conference called "Noise to Signal" for journalists and communications professionals who wanted to learn more about the latest tools and strategies to filter large datasets, social networks and audience metrics into a clear signal for both the Editorial and business side of the news industry. Bundlr founders built a page for news:rewired dedicated to the event: http://bundlr.com/b/news-rewired.[242]

- There is a good demonstration of how Bundlr works on Vimeo: http://vimeo.com/76890542.[243]

- Pretty Girl News is a pg-13 rated Bundle of news about – you guessed it – pretty girls: http://bundlr.com/b/pretty-girl-news

- Anna Paczynska has a lot of nifty bundles that point to a design aesthetic. Wow: http://bundlr.com/b/all-kinds-of-wow[244] Shoes: http://bundlr.com/b/shoes14[245] Furniture http://bundlr.com/b/furni[246]

Bundlr info and Takeaways:

- Bundlr is a cool way to curate and share content.

- The cofounders came up with the idea for Bundlr after attending a conference. They discovered that there wasn't a platform that easily allowed them to share photos, videos and reports, so they created one.[247]

- Bundlr's free accounts have basic capabilities. The premium version is available for $19.95/year.

- The company is based in the founders' hometown, Coimbra, Portugal.

- Although it embodies the characteristics of similar tools, so far no other tool enables real-time updates, collaboration features and the ability to embed pages, which is what the founders believe sets the company apart from its competitors.

- Bundlr's one-step browser button "Bundle This!" is pretty cool and helps the tool standout from the crowd.

Chapter 26: Curation with Social Tools

The need for some sort of method to bring forth the best content on social media platforms is obvious to anyone who works in the social media field, the SEO field or, even, the app industry. Due to the fact that it is often hard for regular engine crawlers to distinguish bunk content from quality content, curation apps and tools are becoming increasingly commonly used by a multitude of different groups to improve user experiences.

Oddly enough, users love to curate their own content, too. Doing this has become much easier, thanks to a number of social media tools and curation apps that have hit a number of different platforms. Below, I provide a general run-through of the most common social tools for curation purposes and how they work in the curation world.

The Major Social Media Platforms – Google+, Facebook, Tumblr, Twitter and Pinterest

Social media platforms are the number one curation tools that you can use, whether you are an individual or a major business. They work primarily by allowing people to share interesting links and photos with their circles, friends' lists and followers. People can reshare content, making quality content increasingly likely to pop up in a person's list of new posts.

Initially, social media platforms were more or less known for being tools to stay in contact with others. However, they've evolved into as a way to share content, photos and videos with others. The most rapidly-evolving aspect of many social media sites is that they are quickly blurring the line between a regular social media site and a content curation tool. For example, Pinterest can be considered both a social media platform as well as a tool for culling poor content, while pushing quality content to the forefront...and it does so in a visually appealing manner, which also helps curation efforts significantly.

With most social media platforms, a frequently reshared post also may end up getting featured as a "popular" or "hot" post sent to everyone. Popularly upvoted posts are also very likely to end up getting similar attention. Meanwhile, posts that are not high quality or not of interest are often left by the wayside to disappear into the myriad other posts.

What makes membership in social media platforms so crucial is that it's truly one of the building blocks of content curation. These platforms are where the bulk of viral content is discovered, how the bulk of customers can be reached and what almost every single content curation tool you'll find is focused on.

Google+

Google+ provides a great social media platform for sharing links, photos, videos and contacts. This particular platform is most well-known for having "circles," which allow you to specifically target your postings and manage which of your contacts gets to see what posts. (Circles are shareable, too.) Google+ is both a visual and textual social media platform.

Getting the Most out of Google+:

- Collect as many circles as you can
- Post publicly
- Share trending material
- Actively seek provocative content and post it regularly
- Share your curation lists and hubs with Google+ or implement Google+ in your hubs and curation lists.

Facebook

Considered the giant of social media, over 1 billion people have a Facebook account. This platform is known for its ability to send messages, having an active notifications feature, being able to make groups as well as company pages and easily use the "Like" button to share content. Like Google+, Facebook allows people to share links, text, photos and videos with little issue, making it both visual and textual in nature.

Facebook is one of the most well-known social media platforms to actively collect data on users and monetize it by displaying ads that are appropriate to the demographics of the user. Company pages, organizational pages and similar pages are allowed to pay for advertising in order to appeal to a wider demographic, which, in turn, allows them to become more likely to have their content furthered by others' curation efforts.

Getting the Most out of Facebook:

- Share unique content through postings on your company site

- Invest in "boosting" posts.

- You can buy Facebook followers, but it is not always advisable.

- Always work toward getting your posts shared and "Liked" heavily. Both increase your chances of having your content end up in other peoples' curation lists, which, in turn, will link back to you.

Twitter

Twitter is a textual social media platform that allows a maximum of 140 characters per post. Primarily used on mobile phones, Twitter has also been used to share links and photographs. It can be implemented in content curation and can also be used as a content curation tool for people who focus on posting items that are all related to a single topic.

Getting the Most out of Twitter:

- Quality content is key, as is interaction.

- Buying Twitter followers can help improve the bottom line of content curation.

- Hashtags can provide curation help and also show trending topics.

Tumblr

Tumblr is a visual social media platform and micro-blogging site that is primarily used for sharing photos and pictures. It is an almost completely visual platform and currently boasts over 201 million blogs. Tumblr is also known for promoting notable blogs and users through its Editorial content as a form of content curation.

Resharing content and networking with major Tumblr users is key to getting followers during your content curation endeavors. Multiple third-party curation tools work on improving Tumblr shares and content curation through the use of a sharable hub.

Pinterest

Pinterest is much like Tumblr in the sense that it is a visual social media platform that focuses on the sharing of photo content. Curation is built into this platform by using collections called "boards" as well as visual bookmarks that are nicknamed "pins." Popular collections are frequently shared through other social media platforms, such as Facebook and Google+.

Getting the Most out of Pinterest

- Multiple analytics tools are available for use to maximize content curation potential.

- It is highly advisable to use a hub content manager for added curation and sharing efforts.

- Adding highly shared, visually appealing content to your curation lists is advisable.

Third-party curation Tools

Third-party curation tools are tools meant to be applied to one or more of the social media platforms previously discussed. They further improve user experiences when viewing content that has been organized on a specific platform and also make it easier for users to share the content on a variety of different platforms. They were not created by the owners of the social media platforms that they were made to be used with.

Juxtapost

Juxtapost is a curation platform that has many things in common with the more well-known Pinterest. Focusing on the visual bookmarking and collection aspect of content curation, Juxtapost works with similar bookmarking functions as well as similar sharing functions for other social media platforms. It also allows users to search for collections that may interest them.

Unlike Pinterest, Juxtapost has private sharing options.

Juxtapost also allows you to export your content to spreadsheets and view it as a hub. Its collaborative tool is exceptional for both marketing, curation and networking. Juxtapost also uses color indexing, special related content features and easy sharing options.

ContentGems

Imagine, if you will, a search engine that is geared toward helping people find quality, inspired content that they can share on their social media platforms. Scanning over 200,000 different feeds every search, ContentGems helps deliver inspiring content for content creators to examine, content collectors to share and services that may be able to help you.

It doesn't only scan typical blogs, either. It also scans for related accounts, users and other social-media related aspects. The results can be shown via the number of shares that they have received as well as the influence that they have had in the past. In order to further curation efforts, the site also allows for one-click shares. Could content sharing get any easier? We think not!

Curalate

Curalate is not a social media platform, but a high-powered visual analytics tool geared toward showing your content curation and social media efforts on four (Instagram, Tumblr, Pinterest and Facebook) of the largest social media platforms on the net. It has a number of different analytics categories, including like2buy, community engagements and social analytics. Each one presents a visual graph explanation of how your curation efforts are working to further your cause.

Curalate is also known for being a tool that is made to make content curation, collection and sharing through a number of platforms instantaneous.

Uberflip

In order to get the best results with curation, grouping your media together can often improve the experience of users who seek out good content. The best way to do this, at least when it comes to doing it using a social media tool, is with Uberflip. By creating an aggregate hub that shows all of your content in an easy-to-share design, users will be more likely to share the content on their own curation tools.

Everything from videos to photos to simple blog posts and ebooks are presented in these sharable hubs, which makes it easier for customers to find the information that they adore. Sharing items on social networking sites is what will drive sales and get your name out there. Also, really, sharing your content is the name of the game when it comes to curation success.

BazaarVoice

In a fashion similar to Uberflip, BazaarVoice works with curation by trying to get customers and viewers to give their two cents on your posts, products and overall social media marketing campaign. This tool not only allows you to curate your own product and company reviews, but also helps you curate your social media campaign in order to have it become a more engaging, inviting and overall successful experience.

BazaarVoice's curation tools focus on content collection and display it in a way that is more user-friendly than the typical experience. Displays often take the shape of an Uberflip-like hub, but can also be put into galleries. In order to further improve curation efforts, BazaarVoice also offers filter tools that can improve user experiences significantly. Most people use BazaarVoice to improve the amount of on-brand content that they have.

PearlTrees

PearlTrees calls itself a "visual and collaborative curation tool" and that is exactly what it is. PearlTrees is a tool that focuses just on much on actually creating and posting content as it does curating it and bringing the best related goodies to the forefront. This particular tool makes it easier to collect content, collaborate with other content creators and see a multitude of different analytics displayed in a visual manner.

Many of the perks of using PearlTrees lies is the fact that it can synchronize multiple platforms and allows people to embed their favorite collections in a number of blog platforms. Clientele who want to increase their shares and expand the number of platforms on which they have their curation endeavors would be wise to use PearlTrees for an added boost.

Chapter 27: Curation with Images /Photos

Content curation is the cornerstone of any modern online marketing approach but it is far from infallible.

With so much data and so many images at our fingertips, it is incredibly easy to poach content from certain corners of the Web. Within this situation arises the potential for copyright infringement and other legal issues which can doom your site indefinitely.

There are several ways to avoid such circumstances – most of which are simple and require a little bit of research:[248]

- Pay royalties for any applicable images you use so that all the images you use are using it in a licensed manner.

- Avoid copyrighted images. Rather than license the images in question, you can instead avoid using such images altogether and instead solely use images that have public domain or creative commons licenses that require no royalty payments

You can also use a reverse image search engine, like TinEye for example, to ensure that the root file of your images does not trace back to a copyrighted piece of content. Paying to use

242

images can be very valuable and worth the investment but it is crucial to know where your content is coming from so that you and your organization do not find themselves in legal trouble.

Like in any industry, there is a code of ethics that comes with using images online that may not belong to you. Sometimes a simple accreditation will be more than enough for the creator of the content that you'd like to use to grant you permission. In order to do this, you must keep three groups in mind:[249] the publisher, the curator and your audience. Appealing to all three subgroups will ensure that you remain out of legal trouble while delivering the best content to your consumers, adding value to your webpage or social media outlet.

US copyright law dictates that "various purposes for which the reproduction of a particular work may be considered fair, such as criticism, comment, news reporting, teaching, scholarship, and research." Section 107 also sets out four factors to be considered in determining whether or not a particular use is fair.[250]

- The purpose and character of the use, including whether such use is of commercial nature or is for nonprofit educational purposes

- The nature of the copyrighted work

- The amount and substantiality of the portion used in relation to the copyrighted work as a whole

- The effect of the use upon the potential market for, or value of, the copyrighted work"

There have been several instances of these copyright laws being unknowingly broken as it is incredibly easy to falter when procuring image content. The social media outlet Pinterest has spawned some legal trouble for a few of its users, [251] for example. These sites naturally rely on the recycling of content in order to generate a user-base that shares and interacts with others based on their "pins" or interests. The style of media is extremely vulnerable to copyright law as it requires only one user to post non-cited content before it can expand and be copied. This leads to a tangled Web of confusion and blame without any tangible trace of who initially broke the law.

Naturally, social media outlets are now becoming wise to copyright laws as sharing and image curation become more common. Outlets like Evernote, Surfmark and other newer media based platforms have integrated a user editing feature to their sites that allow you to accredit, embed and even modify certain content to avoid the legal Web of copyright law.[252] These new social media outlets are on the cutting edge of what will be the future trend in content curation – one that can avoid the associated legal jargon.

This new-found desire to avoid these copyright laws has even given birth to brand new consensual photo sharing apps like Cluster, which actually feeds on the goodwill of users to give their content away. Users upload their content to select categories allowing others to access them via cloud computing. Consensually giving away your original content is part of the sign-up conditions so that legal affairs can be left behind without worry.[253]

These new and exciting trends are a revolutionary period in media marketing and will allow the fluidity of image curation to endure through what could have been a shaky period. Markets will find new ways to re-invent themselves and remain relevant so long as they stay within the confines of the law.

Part 5

Curation in the Wild

Chapter 28: Curation for Brand Marketers/Content Marketing

For brands, the advent of social media has turned conventional marketing upside-down. No longer can brands simply buy their way into the conversation with the largest media megaphone. As we know, authenticity is critical. So, in this new world of curated content, the big brand question is "What in the world should I tweet about?" The balance of self-referential social messaging with curated content is one that needs to be carefully calculated. Too many self-referential links or pointers and you're likely to come off as vain and self-important. Too much reliance on outside Editorial and social content and it'll seem like you're just coasting along, taking your fans and customers along on a free ride. The goal is to be part of the conversation, not to either monopolize it or lurk in the background.

Tristian Handy is a social media marketer who turned up some pretty solid research on this topic. He asked the question: "Isn't promoting your own content akin to talking about yourself? And isn't that rude, and thus ineffective?" He analyzed more than 150,000 social media posts to test that assumption. [254] The sample included tweets and status updates from more than 1,000 Twitter, Facebook and LinkedIn customers who were, typically, professional marketers representing a range of company sizes across most major industries.

The question that Handy asked was, "Which works best, curation or creation?" His answer: "When looking at clicks, curation clearly dominates. Posts linking to third-party sites generate 33% more clicks than posts linking to owned sites. This makes sense — the very best content on the Internet is typically not going to live at yourcompany.com. But the choice isn't really between creation and curation — you should be doing both. The question is really what mix of those two strategies you should employ for maximum clicks and conversions?"

Curators = Companies that link to third-party sites 75% or more of the time.

Table #1[255]

Clicks per Post	Click-to-Conversion Rate	Conversions per Post
47.8	.2%	.10

Companies in this group focus very heavily on curation and rarely, if ever, link to their own content. The results bear this out as they generate a lot of clicks, but very few conversions.

Balanced = Companies that link to third-party sites 50% to 75% of the time.

Table #2[256]

Clicks per Post	Click-to-Conversion Rate	Conversions per Post
38.4	2.5%	.95

Companies in this group employ a balanced strategy of content creation and content curation. Their clicks per post are lower than curators, but they generate significantly more conversions.

Self-Promoters = Companies that link to their own content 50% or more of the time.

Table #3[257]

Clicks per Post	Click-to-Conversion Rate	Conversions per Post
17.0	2.4%	.41

Companies in this group link to their own content a majority of the time, which negatively impacts their clicks per post. This reduction isn't made up by an increased conversion rate.

It's clear from the data that companies in the Balanced category achieve the best results overall. They generate 20% fewer clicks per post than curators, but their conversion rate is 10 times higher. I'll take that trade any day.

The Creation and curation Sweet Spot

We've already determined that linking to your site 25% to 50% of the time generates the best results, but what if we look at the practices of the top five companies in generating clicks and conversions? What are they doing that has been so effective for them?

The top five companies in his sample that generated the most clicks linked to their own sites 37.9% of the time. These companies generated conversions links to their own sites 41.6% of the time, which feels like a pretty solid, sweet spot.

Lessons Learned and Takeaways

After digging into the numbers, the optimal balance for most companies is to link to their own content between 25% and

50% of the time, with 40% being the ideal mark. However, beware of the law of averages! Just because these numbers are true overall does not mean that they are the best numbers for you. Outliers exist.

Chapter 29: Curation for Education

Learning 2.0 – Content Curation

In examining how we consume information online and through mobile devices, we soon realize how critical the methods of content curation are in knowledge building. At any given moment, we're scanning or scrutinizing multiple sources, taking a chunk here and a chunk there before moving on with the information residue, whatever bits are retained in our memory. Not merely a forward-looking concept, in practice content curation can preserve our ability to absorb and master the flow of information, enhance our intelligence as technology consumers, and compete on a global scale as systems of learning continue to evolve.

By its simplest definition, content curation is "the gathering, organizing and online presentation of content related to a particular theme or topic."[258]

An excellent, comprehensive article by Robin Good, "Why curation Will Transform Education and Learning," covers ten essential reasons for curation's influence on systematic courses of learning and diagnoses the future of the "educational ecosystem"[259] that continues to dismantle more traditional institutions. In fact, Good believes these institutions will soon become obsolete.[260]

Good cuts to the core of what he calls "fast food information consumption" and what he sees as its downward trend. Rather than the rapid accumulation of facts and data via search giants like Google, we're being pushed into "learning how to learn" as Good describes it, by seeking out and identifying more refined elements of information we wish to absorb, build on and share. Content curation offers a more engaged, interactive and personalized style of learning. Its multi-dimensional applications allow us to be far more participatory and savvy by applying our own discernment. We're not just digesting recycled information, we're analyzing its value. Citing digital literacy skill (e.g., the use of software and applications), Good emphasizes the importance of applying such skills to aid in this process of assessing, qualifying and organizing content.[261]

As cited by Good, the increase of "open" teaching/learning content hubs points to the ever-growing presence of and need for curated content. Rapid growth of open content resources, such as "Open Culture," where users have access to hundreds of free online courses from universities around the country, is restructuring the educational system.[262] Transcending the textbook, these forums are structured around the sharing of new information, filtering out old ideas from outdated platforms and incorporating modern perspectives in a topic of study. A college campus being the prerequisite access to higher learning is a thing of the past. Online learning hubs facilitate blended learning through extended networks that go beyond the walls of a classroom and into global learning communities.

In the traditional classroom setting, teachers are curating their textbooks, taking what they perceive as the most effectively harnessed subject matter and offering their students an upgraded version of classroom learning.

Another reason Good lists for curation being the pathway to our future is our changing job market.[263] No longer can workers rest on the old-school credential of a diploma or certificate as their voucher for qualification. Today's environment demands workers adopt a more wide-ranging skill set in order to compete in a job market that's connected with and propelled by technology. In the business world, individualized roles or areas of expertise are being viewed in relationship to each other rather than segmented parts. Workers will need to be knowledgeable in several areas, access those areas through new avenues of information sharing, and have a broader awareness of how their specific role interplays within a larger framework in order to replicate the structure of the virtual world through interconnectedness.

The tenth, but by no means least important reason on Good's list is the demand for trusted guidance.[264] With "overflow" or "overload," no matter how you label it, we're faced with a tsunami of information every time we connect to the virtual learning space. In many instances, that means we're processing diluted, dated and generic information. In other cases, we come across disinformation that gets flung around the Internet with false authority. Whatever the case, it's up to us as agents of learning to be astute about what's being processed in all of the noise, whether it holds value, and how that information is incorporated into our knowledge base in more actionable, less static ways. Those individuals who invest their time and resources in becoming expert curators (e.g., teachers) will have an undeniable advantage in this 21st century of learning.

Teachers and curation

In her article, "curation in the Classroom," Nancy White discusses 21st century skills to better educate students. An open advocate, White mentions a grant she manages that aims to ensure students acquire and go into the classroom equipped with 21st century skills. [265] Interestingly, White questions what it means to curate and its ultimate value in learning as the "definition of curating seems to have no boundaries."[266] White closely examines how curation, when put into practice in the classroom, can have measurable effects for both teachers and students.

Using a diagram, White shows a pyramid structure that reflects levels of learning with "knowledge" at its base and "evaluation" at the top, indicating that informed appraisal of what's being taught is one of the primary goals of classroom curation. There are several steps in between before reaching the evaluation phase. White remarks that some information gathering is void of "deep thinking," where the collector isn't imbuing any appreciation for the pieces being assembled or why they're on the table so to speak. In White's estimation, the "inquiry process" is an integral part of the curating process in education. [267] Deciding what's included versus what's discarded engages deep thinking and meaningful discussion, while elevating the process to the synthesizing of information, one level below evaluation.

Synthesizing information instills relevancy and a closer examination of why it merits a place in what's being taught in the classroom. White is aligned with this type of "deep thinking" and circles back to a more clarified perspective on the purposes of curation in the classroom. It eliminates a one-sided venue where students are lectured and creates a comprehensive experience where students are encouraged to become curators themselves. "Participatory learning leads to increased understanding."[268]

Curation Tools

1. CurationSoft

CurationSoft is an all-in-one tool through which site owners can incorporate value-added content to their site by scanning and pulling information from the Web that Internet users are looking for and then post it on their sites, allowing them to be the "go-to" source for information. Instead of weeding through numerous search results, CurationSoft serves as a shortcut and the system allows curators to easily populate their sites with value-added content. This bumps up the owner's site in the search ranks on Google (the desired goal) as their site becomes qualified as a primary resource/expert authority. [269] High-quality, fresh content is the driving message in the CurationSoft intro video as it underscores the increasing demand for updated content. Users can take old content and reconfigure it into new content to drive users to their page, elevating their reputability.

The software allows users to search keywords to source content that will drive traffic to their site. Post Builder helps simplify blogging as site owners can post to more than one blog simultaneously.

The software is designed to be interchangeable with WordPress, so, if need be, site owners can go straight to CurationSoft and bypass WordPress. You can also scan RSS feeds and add them to CurationSoft before pulling curated content from those feeds. Generating high-quality posts increases traffic and spikes your relevance score as the program allows for premium content to be streamlined through your site on a consistent basis.[270] That content is then layered with and enhanced by owner commentary, giving it a fresh presentation and unique spin. CurationSoft has a list of outlets, such as Google Blogs, Google News and Wikipedia from which site owners can source.

Curation Soft Takeaways:

- A course in Internet 2.0, CurationSoft has tapped into the market of independent, information-driven sites that require supplementation of fresh, user-valued content to position themselves as viable, high-ranking resources.

- It's a valuable teaching tool for anyone who wants to stay informed about where the flow of information is headed.

- Ultimately, this program is best suited for site owners, those who brand themselves as experts in their field or newbie bloggers looking to increase readership.

2. Diigo Education Edition

Described as a "cloud-based personal management system" on their homepage, Diigo was initially designed as an online bookmarking tool.[271] Over the years, it has progressed into an interactive learning and project-sharing forum. Diigo allows users to collect information via its various search tools and store them in a virtual library or the Diigo Cloud, which can be accessed through any mobile device that the site supports. You can add digital highlights and interactive sticky notes. When information is highlighted from a Webpage, Diigo allows you to return to that page on any device and pick up where you left off. To use the program a Diigo toolbar is installed into the browser. Then, sites can be bookmarked through the browser using tags for easy search/reference. You can also annotate information on webpages to keep track of reference notes.

Another cool feature is "snapshot," through which you can archive Webpages so that, if that site becomes inactive or is removed, it's stored in Diigo. You can also read pages offline via Diigo as well as take notes and pictures for ideas you want to store.[272]

Diigo provides a forum for project-based learning for students. Structured with an education domain and educator accounts, teachers can organize classes for K-12 students as well as higher education students. Teachers can create student accounts for an entire class where students are automatically set up to start using the site for online research, note sharing and interactive learning.

Diigo Takeaways:

- With seven million registered users that include law firms, marketing agencies, consultants, recruiters, Web designers, researchers, students and teachers... anyone who does a lot of knowledge-oriented information consumption can make use of Diigo.[273]

- Diigo is a great tool for teachers who are developing interactive, hands-on learning experiences in the classroom.

- It's also a great tool for professionals who want to organize project development and keep track of ideas, stories and reference information.

3. Dipity

Dipity allows users to create a virtual timeline of "useful information" from the Internet that is extracted from social media, search engines and selected sites. This timeline contains information on world events, figures in history or studied subjects.

Users build timelines to recreate cultural/historical events.[274] The site attracts a varied group of users. For example, a journalist wrote about using Dipity to present a timeline on the Fukushima disaster.[275] It places the subject matter in a unique context where the chronicling of events through the use of multimedia gives it tangibility.

Timelines are built with piece-meal images, titles and descriptions. Users can modify timelines by adding their own researched material. Content can be imported from various sites, such as YouTube, with video clips that inform the topic's chronology. Each description must be tagged with a complete date (i.e., month, day and year).[276] Users can modify the theme or display of their timelines, apply permissions for comments and so on. Content imported into timelines can be retrieved from social media sites such as Flickr, Vimeo and Facebook. [277] A perfect teaching tool, Dipity is used by students and teachers for shared learning and creative implementation with hands-on, creative education. Dipity gives its users an opportunity to be virtual authors of their favorite subjects, fostering renewed interest and discussion.

Dipity Takeaways:

- Dipity is a snapshot of the evolution of traditional methods of education, making it an inviting experimental tool for teachers. [278]

- Participatory learning is a valued method for educators who want to maintain an active, engaged learning environment.

- The site is best used for building and sharing information on social, cultural or historical events.

- Its users are primarily educators, graduate school students and professionals.[279]

4. Evernote

Evernote is your virtual notepad, project file or to-do list. A storage house for files, notes, projects ideas, bookmarked sites, photos and travel itineraries, users can also share their work. It also has a feature where you can record audio. The Evernote Web Clipper keeps your bookmarks, notes and images in one place.

There's a Tips and Stories page on the site with informative blog posts, such as tips to keep more organized, the most effective way to collect content for your Evernote account, the best use of the Evernote apps and guidance on sharing Notebooks on the site. "Share Your Knowledge with Evernote" guides users on sharing information through Notebooks. Notebooks are created to store curated information and then the Notebook's creator can invite friends to view or modify its contents.[280] Before sharing, you can predetermine "sharing permissions" for people on your friends list. For example, you might allow a close colleague to add to or modify the contents of a notebook, while a virtual friend can only view the information.

A unique feature on the site is "Evernote Hello," where you can keep a log of the people you've met, access images of faces and revisit shared experiences. Evernote is being used as a classroom tool where teachers can create notebooks for class projects, giving students learning resources, project blogs and an outlet to exchange thoughts about the project's progress.[281]

Evernote Takeaways:

- An effective blend of social networking, knowledge sharing and task organization, Evernote hits the bull's-eye in terms of bridging networks of educators, business people and creative thinkers.

- The site is a great companion tool for entrepreneurs who want to keep a record of new ideas or work on projects with clients and colleagues.

5. eLearning Tags

A hub for educational technology, eLearning Tags is a social bookmarking site where educators and students can share and vote on eLearning content, such as social learning, gamification, infographics and LMS (Learning Management System).[282] According to an article by Karla Gutierrez, "18 Mind-Blowing eLearning Statistics You Need to Know," eLearning is the second most important training method within organizations.[283]

On the site, users post descriptions of eLearning tools and the community votes on the usefulness of the information. There's also a menu that tracks top stories, upcoming news and user comments. In the far right margin is a reference list of the top five contributors and users that notes the consistent, high-quality information that they contribute to the site.[284] The site interfaces with social media sites and has a number of tips and tricks for smart use of these sites. For example, the site contains an in-depth tutorial on the most effective, market-savvy use of a Twitter hashtag.[285]

eLearning Tags Takeaways:

- Today's student or professional, regardless of demographic background, would be wise to learn how to use eLearning Tags. It's a tremendous resource of information on the latest in technology education.

- Gutierrez's article points out that, along with Europe, the US accounts for over 70% of the global eLearning industry and that eLearning is "proven to increase knowledge retention by 25% to 60%."[286]

6. Symbaloo

Symbaloo is a very simple, straightforward service that organizes your favorite sites and accumulated bookmarks into one interface.[287] Using a personalized start page arranged into a thumbnail palette, users can access their favorite places with just one click. Also available on almost any mobile device, the site allows quick navigation through your personalized landscape of frequently visited sites. This set-up bypasses the step of typing in the full URL into the navigation bar, appealing to almost anyone who spends time on the Web.

Symbaloo Takeaways:

- This site is a sensible solution for those looking to cut down on search time and is also popular with the hyper-organized who can gather their favorite places into a condensed, simplified-navigation format.

Chapter 30: Curation for Fashion

Before the invention of the Internet, department stores, shopping malls and strip malls ruled the retail universe. However, with the growing popularity of the Web and the advent of mobile apps, the gap between brick-and-mortar shops and online stores is steadily closing.

An obvious advantage exists to a brick-and-mortar shops over online stores – instant gratification. Consumers don't have to sit at home waiting impatiently for the UPS man to come and avoid scowling at those annoying yellow and brown notes when a bathroom break or trip to the corner store is needed. "While the Internet has been very effective at competing on price, it has not yet cracked the code of how to affordably get products to the end consumer on the same day they are purchased,"[288] Randy Anderson, head of CBRE Research, Americas, said in an interview with WPC News.

Additionally, consumers have the ability to touch, feel and really try on gear, which cuts down on trips to the post office to return unwanted items. Conversely, digital rivals are able to offer larger selections to consumers around the world and the shops are open 24/7/365. If Amazon has its way, it would, at least, be able to offer same-day service without the same-day service costs.

- Forty percent of shoppers spent more than they planned while shopping brick-and-mortar as opposed to the 25% of online shoppers who spent more than anticipated.

- Ecommerce has been making significant headway over the last decade. In 2004, ecommerce accounted for only 25% of retail sales.[289] In the decade since, those numbers have jumped to 31%,[290] with Amazon leading the way.

- Amazon earnings for Q4 of 2013 sales increased 20% to $25.59 billion.

- During the third quarter, total retail sales increased 4.7% year-over-year. In comparison, ecommerce sales increased by a much higher 18.2% during the same time period.[291]

Ecommerce Fashion Curation:

Ecommerce retail companies have sprouted exponentially over the past several years. Fashion savvy consumers have a cornucopia of options. Here are five online curated marketplaces that are making a lot of good Internet 'noise.'

GLANCE by Zappos

Zappos is an ecommerce site that made a splash by offering designer footwear at discount price. It later expanded its product line to include apparel, accessories and housewares. According to *Fast Company,* the online giant boasts an inventory containing over 127,000 styles and over 1,000 brands.[292]

Realizing that those numbers can befuddle wary shoppers, the company introduced GLANCE, a social commerce app that allows shoppers to discover products from Zappos through curated collections. The app also allows uses to "heart" products they love and discover products that fellow shoppers heart as well.

Prior to working for Zappos Labs, Will Young, the director of Zappos Labs, was a programmer acting as an independent consultant for several companies. He's also a general partner at a Vegas tech fund, VegasTechFund, which is a seed stage investment fund focused on investing in founders and startups solving huge problems. The investors are committed to building a vibrant, connected tech community in downtown Las Vegas. Young received his education at the University of British Columbia.

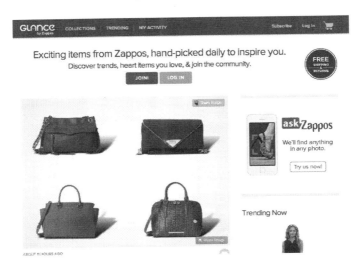

Today, Zappos has revenues in excess of $1 billion.[293] Zappos Labs is headquartered in San Francisco. Zappos is headquartered in Las Vegas.

Mission of the Company

Similar to many apps of its kind, Glance aims to remove the Internet clutter and noise, making it easier for Zappos shoppers to shop. "The products and the people are heroes here," said Carrie Whitehead, Zappos' product and UX manager.[294]

How It Works

Items are hand-curated daily and uploaded to the site. Users are then able to purchase collections and individual items or save them for later purchase. Hearted items are displayed for everyone to see, thus encouraging users to purchase items hearted by their peers.

Zappos GLANCE Takeaways

- Zappos filled a void in the marketplace and, initially, became super successful with footwear before expanding.

- It realized that its success created another problem of providing too many options for consumers. Glance is its solution to clearing the clutter.

- Zappo Labs is a San Francisco-based in-house think tank created in 2012 just to come up with innovated ways to stay relevant in the digital age.

- Glance isn't Zappos first crack at social networking. Several years ago, it launched My.Zappos, which has since been shuttered. Trying to capitalize off of the Twitter craze, it launched Tweetwall, which also failed to make significant waves.

FANCY

Fancy is a social commerce app that allows users to discover and buy items curated by its global community of subscribers. Part photo sharing and part store, fancy is not exclusively used for curating fashion, but that is a huge component.

Business Insider said that it's "the social version of Amazon. It's like Pinterest, but with a heavier emphasis on ecommerce."[295] What really separates Fancy from Pinterest is the ability to like and purchase curated items.

Mission of the Company

In an interview Fancy founder Joseph Einhorn said that he wasn't just looking to create another cool app; he wanted to build something useful with staying power. "First, there was Tumblr, where you see a cool image of something  and then you have a dead-end. Then, there's Pinterest, which is similar, and then there's us, but we have a price tag. We've been laser-focused on stuff you can really buy and places you can actually visit or experience, but it's based on the social curation that users already know how to do from these other sites. Think about us in the way you think of Amazon. They've done a lot of amazing things that other people haven't done or aren't able to do. The difference is that we believe searching is an old way to do commerce, and that our kind of discovery in the stream is the new way."[296]

At the age of 16, Fancy founder and CEO Joseph Einhorn created his first startup, Capital IQ, a corporate information service. In 2004, he served as CTO of Inform Technologies before going on to found Fancy in 2009.

How it works

The community of Fancy users are, in essence, the curators. In order to contribute, users employ the bookmarklet tool. When interesting things are discovered, they can be selected, described and added to personal feeds, which is automatically linked back to the original page.

Fancy Box

Fancy Box is a monthly subscription service for which users pay $39 to receive a box full of different products available from Fancy, worth an estimated total of $80 or more. Fancy allows for boxes to be customized by category, such as men, women, home, gadgets, media and more.

Gifting

Fancy helps users obtain gift ideas through their "Gift" tab. Users can either send a Fancy Box worth $60 or browse for gift ideas by color or price, ranging from $1 to $500+. Fancy also offers gift guides, such as Back to School, For Him, Anniversary and Winter Getaways. Finally, users can view recommendations for gifts by sending in a customized description of what they desire and the individual designated to receive the gift.

Promotions

Users receive a credit of $1 for every friend who signs up and $10 when that friend buys something within 60 days.[297]

Examples of Use

Business Insider provided a great visual of how the app works:http://www.businessinsider.com/the-fancy-app-guide-2012-8?op=1.[298]

Fancy Takeaways

- Fancy is 100% user-curated.

- It has a large celebrity user-base.

- Fancy has taken the best parts of many social networking sites, such as Amazon and Pinterest, and improved upon those sites to create a more enhanced shopping and social networking experience for users.

- In the case of Amazon, Fancy doesn't quash the need for the Internet giant, but, in many ways, it can be viewed as a cool, distant cousin.

- In 2012, Apple was in talks of acquiring the company; the acquisition was never completed.

AHAlife

Born out of founder and CEO Shauna Mei's love of travel and well-crafted niche items, [299] AHAlife.com is a discovery shopping destination for curated lifestyle products that span fashion, design, technology, media, food, beauty and travel. Many commerce curation sites exist, but *TechCrunch* writer Leena Rao says AHAlife stands out from the rest. "What makes the site compelling is the blend of content, commerce and curation in AHAlife's platform."[300]

The site boasts many celebrity curators, such as Project Runway's Tim Gunn, fashion designer Donna Karan and media magnate Tina Brown.

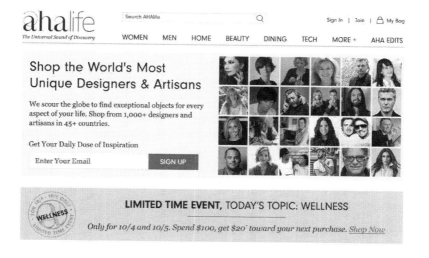

In addition to founding AHAlife, Mei established Mobius Strip, LLC, a company dedicated to creating responsible, inspiring and profitable businesses at the intersection between fashion/design and life's experiences. She also served as the CEO of Casall International, a Swedish wellness/active-wear company based in Stockholm. Prior to Casall, Mei co-founded Aronsson Group, a luxury fashion investment and advisory firm, with Jeffry Aronsson (former CEO of Donna Karan International, Marc Jacobs and Oscar de la Renta). They invested in and advised many companies from fashion brands such as Matthew Williamson, to trading companies, such as Mitsui. Mei worked in both private equity (principal investment area) and investment banking at Goldman Sachs, where she worked on several deals in the fashion-media space, most notably the sale of the Neiman Marcus Group.

An MIT graduate with a double major in Electrical Engineering and Computer Science, Mei concentrated on Artificial Intelligence and Management Finance.

Mission of the company

The company aims to "Empower designers, artisans and innovators to thrive online and connect people around the world."[301] Mei said that the company "focuses on quality, not quantity of items sold on the site and aims to help customers cut through the noise."[302]

How does it work?

AHAlife discovers new products through the AHAlife curators, the New York-based AHAlife team, and from site members who are also able to become curators for the site by submitting potential products. Much like Gilt.com and Woot!, a new hand-selected item is posted every day and emailed to AHAlife subscribers. Curated items are instantly available for purchase directly from the site. Unlike many daily deal sites, items on AHAlife are available for an indefinite amount of time. So, in case you decide to take a tech sabbatical and power down for a few days (nearly impossible today), you can rest knowing Monday's AHA item can be purchased Friday night.

AHAlife info and Takeaways

- AHAlife was conceived on a plane from Stockholm.

- AHAlife provides a platform for consumers to purchase luxury items curated by well-respected individuals in the world of fashion, entertainment and business.

- Independent designers and artisans are given a platform to sell their wares. Everybody wins and, with the ability to submit curated items, everybody can also be an expert.

- Membership is free.

- The company has 45 employees and is based in New York's Soho neighborhood.

- It acquired photo-sharing site Kaptur last year because Mei said "that Kaptur's viral expertise[303] [was] what [the] company needed to expand its user-base."

- The company owns AHAnoir, a site devoted to intimate objects, aka sex toys.

Thrillist

"Girls Just Want to Have Fun" was the shero warrior call spawned by Cyndi Lauper's 80's hit. Apparently, boys wanna have fun too, and the founders of Thrillist wanna assist in the revelry.

Thrillist is a leading men's digital lifestyle brand, providing all that's new, unknown or under-appreciated in food, drink, entertainment, nightlife, gadgets and fashion.

Thrillist started off as a daily email newsletter informing men where to party, eat and shop, but with the 2010 acquisition of Jackthreads, a members-only flash sale site for men's fashions, it soon grew to become a baby Amazon in the making.[304]

Thrillist has a niche audience made up of young, hip, urban men with an edgy sense of humor and a keen sense of fashion, who like to have a good time. They are more Jimmy Fallon and Conan O'Brien than Jay Leno and David Letterman. The Thrillist writing matches the audience. Subscribers once received a daily deal for "a strip and an strip" – a dance at the strip club Scores and a steak at its in-house restaurant.[305]

In addition to co-founding and being CEO of Thrillist, Ben Lerer is the managing director at Lerer Ventures, a seed stage venture capital fund started by his father, Ken Lerer, the cofounder of *The Huffington Post.* .

Adam Rich, is the cofounder and Editor-in-chief of Thrillist.com. He oversees all of the Editorial content for the newsletter. Originally from California, Rich graduated from the University of Pennsylvania in 2002 before moving to New

York City to work in software development for Viewpoint Corp., a leading provider of Web technologies.

Thrillist is available in 23 cities with an additional 21 on the way. It is headquartered in New York City. It was named #15 on the *Forbes "Most Promising Companies"* list.[306]

Company Mission

To keep young, urban men in the loop by unearthing interesting foods, places, activities and gear.

How It Works

Thrillist is a quick, free, daily email. Each weekday, Thrillist will drop subscribers a must-have recommendation from the best of what's new to deeply under-the-radar goodness. As they describe it: "talking absinthe-only cocktail spots, eateries that dish up BBQ Rattlesnake Salad and Reindeer in Bourbon Sauce, and ATMs whose currency is marijuana - handy, although after making a withdrawal, you'll feel even more paranoid about the stocking repercussions of consuming Santa's only friend."[307]

Thrillist says it only covers what it likes and promises: "We're not going to waste our time or yours with things that suck - you already have your job for that. So, we don't write reviews, just recommendations, and because we painstakingly wade through the crap to unearth greatness, you get exclusively the best of your city's food, drinks, gear, services, entertainment, travel options and events, like booze cruises, and a divine concept surely birthed on a booze cruise - stripper cruises."[308]

Being the Internet behemoth that it is, Amazon continues to have a big fat target on its back and entrepreneurs are always cooking up ways to defeat Goliath. In an interview with _Fortune,_ Ben Lerer explained his ingredients for success. "By having things that Amazon doesn't have. At Thrillist, we sell you stuff you need that you can't find anywhere else. Almost half of what we sell is exclusive to us, with a big portion of that stuff actually being made by us. You can't price-check an item on Amazon that they don't cover. Plus, fashion is a category that is particularly tough for a company like Amazon that is so focused on the Commerce 1.0 model. Inspiration isn't in its DNA, and it thinks about curation as something that an algorithm does, not a brand or a person. This is counter to what social media is all about, and people who are raised on social media don't only want an algorithm telling them what they should buy. They want to trust the brands that sell them things, and fashion is a category that Amazon doesn't have trust in."[309]

They've also been successful by taking the party offline. In June 2014, the company hosted its second annual Best Day of

Your Life, a curated event where attendees were able to party, eat and purchase items typically only available on the site.[310]

Thrillist info and takeaways

- Thrillist can be taken at face value: it's for men of a certain demographic – young, hip, urban, edgy, fashionable – and it has succeeded in catering to that group.

- The founders are all about exploring the best that the city has to offer. They've maintained their original passion and have since expanded and turned it into a real, thriving ecommerce/publishing business.

ShoeDazzle

ShoeDazzle is an online fashion subscription service co-founded by reality starlet Kim Kardashian. The company debuts a monthly selection of shoes, handbags and jewelry and provides its members with a showroom curated by fashion experts to their indicated fashion preferences.

Celebrity Stylist Rachel Zoe replaced Kim Kardashian as the ShoeDazzle chief stylist and assumed the sole responsibility for picking shoe styles, curating a monthly boutique and doling out fashion advice to ShoeDazzle customers.

Mission

According to the company's site, ShoeDazzle was "founded on the belief that every woman deserves access to on-trend, quality shoes that fit her style."[311]

How it works

Every month, the ShoeDazzle fashion team — led by chief stylist Rachel Zoe — offers their clients personalized shoe, handbag and accessory recommendations. Clients also enjoy access to exclusive boutiques, new arrivals throughout each month and award-winning client services.

Once a membership is established, a subscriber has to complete a personal profile. Then, within 24 hours, the first showroom filled with shoes and handbags is ready. Members will also get access to SD stylist-curated boutiques and lookbooks, which feature the latest trends and edits.

ShoeDazzle also provides expert styling, so that members can indulge their love of fashion and get advice from the pros. Their stylists keep members in the loop on what's hot in shoes, handbags and jewelry, as well as how to wear them to stay on-trend and in season.

Shopping at ShoeDazzle is free. For clients who want the VIP experience, with benefits like free shipping and members-only pricing, the company offers a VIP Elite Membership for $39.95 a month, which goes straight into subscriber accounts to spend as a VIP Credit.[312]

Each month chief stylist Rachel Zoe offers style advice and curates a selection of shoes and handbags.

Leadership

Kim Kardashian may seem like just another pretty-faced reality show babe (well, she kinda is), but she's also turned out to be a pretty smart businesswoman. In addition to co-founding ShoeDazzle, Kardashian has attached her image to many products, the most recent being the hot-selling app Kim Kardashian: Hollywood.[313] *Forbes* estimates that the addictive mobile game, developed by Glu Games, will bring in $200 million dollars by the end of 2014.[314]

Kardashian is the daughter of famed attorney Robert Kardashian (part of OJ Simpson's team) and Kris Jenner. She first became a tabloid fixture as the best friend of fellow socialite Paris Hilton. Kardashian went on to make a name for herself after a 2007 sex tape she made with singer Ray J hit the market. From there, she starred in several reality shows capitalizing off of her fame and notoriety, including *Keeping Up with the Kardashians* and *Kourtney and Kim Take New York*. A 2011 marriage to basketball player Kris Humphries drew heavy criticism, as the lavish televised nuptials produced a union that only lasted 72 days. Kardashian married rap star Kanye West this year; they have a one-year-old daughter named North.

Brian Lee is the cofounder and CEO of ShoeDazzle as well as the cofounder and CEO of The Honest Company, Inc. He is also the cofounder of BAM Ventures. Formerly an attorney with Skadden, Arps, Slate, Meagher & Flom, LLP and a manager at Deloitte & Touche, LLP, he co-founded LegalZoom in 2001 and served as its co-president. He also serves as a member of the advisory board at Bouju, Inc. and sits on the board of the Lowell Milken Institute of Business Law and Policy at UCLA School of Law as well as the Los Angeles Youth Network. He has substantial experience in consulting on tax and accounting issues, specializing in the high technology industry. He earned the distinction as one of the 25 Most Notable Korean-American Entrepreneurs by Forbes in 2009. Lee received his J.D. from the UCLA School of Law in 1996 and graduated magna cum laude with a B.A. in Business and Economics from UCLA.

In addition to co-founding ShoeDazzle, Robert Shapiro also co-founded LegalZoom with Brian Lee. He is most famously known for successfully defending OJ Simpson and Marlon Brando's son, Christian Brando.

ShoeDazzle info and Takeaways

- If you're a woman (or man) who loves pretty shoes, ShoeDazzle is a good fit.

- On-screen star power and behind-the-scene business acumen helped to establish the company as a winner in the ecommerce subscription service arena.

- Now with famed fashion stylist Rachel Zoe curating its styles, it's sure to thrive for many fiscal quarters to come.

Brick-and-mortar shops

Below are a couple of popular brick-and-mortar shops and a boutique store that are taking fashion and fashion curation to exciting heights.

H&M

H&M is a Swedish retail-clothing company with stores in 53 countries. In 2004, the company began to offer curated collections by famous designers, such as Karl Lagerfeld,[315] Versace[316] and Stella McCartney.[317]

H&M info and Takeaways

- H&M opened its first store in Västerås, Sweden, selling women's clothing in 1947. The store was called Hennes.

- In 1968, founder Erling Persson acquired Maurtize Widforss, a hunting and fishing equipment store. The store began to sell men's and children's clothing. The store name changed to Hennes & Mauritz.

- In 2000, H&M opened its first store on 5th Avenue in New York City and soon after launched a store in Spain.[318]

Target

In 2012, Target Corp introduced a pilot program <u>The Shops of Target</u>, which featured a curated collection of boutiques from around the country. Participating shops included such trendsetting boutique retailers as the Webster in Miami, Privet House in Connecticut and The Candy Store in San Francisco.[319] The shops aren't currently operating, but, in a Facebook message to me, Target's Facebook moderator Jennifer said: "Thanks so much for asking! At this time, we don't have plans for a future "flight" of the Shops at Target, but we do have a number of collaborations planned for 2014 and beyond. Stay tuned for details! Have a great day!"

Target info and Takeaways

- The first Target opened in 1962 in Roseville, MN

- The nickname "Tar-zhay" was coined with the debut of the first store.

- Target team members first donned the red and khaki-colored uniforms in 1993.

- Since 2012, Target's community-based initiates have totaled more than $4 million each week.

Curate Boutique

Curate Boutique is a brick-and-mortar store located in the Hyde Park section of Cincinnati, Ohio. The company bills itself as the place to shop for the "freshest, most unique designs."

How It Works

In-store customers are able to sift through 'Style Collections,' which provide a curated experience. According to the company site, Founder Courtney PeGan said each collection has a story: "The idea behind "Style Collections" was born because PeGan wanted to highlight emerging fashion trends and house very different styles and aesthetics under one roof, but with some semblance of order. These Style Collections enable shoppers to know the story behind why each piece was chosen and how it fits within a broader trend, style. These highly curated collections will be released each season to highlight evolving trends and styles."[320]

Curate Boutique info and Takeaways

- The store features fashionable items made by local artisans and national designers.

- Nothing in the store is over $300 and most items are under $200!

- Founded in 2013, the company launched its online store a year later by popular demand.

Five Innovative Fashion curators

Andrew Bolton

"The power of fashion lies in its power to transform identity. So, I try to fit in ideas with the zeitgeist."[321]

As the curator of the Metropolitan Museum of Art's Costume Institute since 2006, Andrew Bolton is recognized for having spearheaded some of the most groundbreaking and innovative fashion exhibitions in the museum's history. Most noted for the phenomenally successful 'Alexander McQueen: Savage Beauty' retrospective in 2011, Bolton has also overseen 'Dangerous Liaisons' and 'AngloMania: Tradition and Transgression in British Fashion.'

A graduate of anthropology from the University of East Anglia, Bolton spent 10 years at the Victoria & Albert Museum in London before decamping for New York. A celebrated curator, Bolton has been awarded the 'Best Design Show' award by the International Association of Art Critics for an exhibition on couturier Paul Poiret. In 2009, Bolton was awarded the AIGA Design Award and the Independent Publisher Book Award for 'Superheroes: Fashion and Fantasy' catalogue.

Olivier Saillard

"More than ever, our role as museums is to show authors and not advertising initiatives."[322]

This past fall, Olivier Saillard was deemed "the man of the hour" by *WWD*. Saillard is one of fashion's premier historians and curators. He has curated some of the most innovative and exclusive fashion exhibitions at the Musée de la Mode in Paris and Marseille, the Musée Bordelle and the Victoria & Albert Museum in London. Most noted for his critically acclaimed '*Madame Grès*' exhibition in 2011, Saillard also curated the '*Comme des Garçons: White Drama*' retrospective and the '*Balenciaga Fashion Collector*' exhibition at the Les Docks. He also Cite de la Mode et du Design in 2012 and staged the live performance art exhibition *The Impossible Wardrobe*, featuring relics worn by Marie Antoinette, Napoleon and Elsa Schiaperelli in collaboration with Tilda Swinton at the Palais de Tokyo. Saillard was appointed as director of the Musée Galliera Paris in 2010. The historic museum, which has been closed for renovations since 2010, re-opened in September 2013 with an Azzedine Alaïa retrospective curated by Saillard.

Saillard studied archaeology and contemporary art in Besançon, eastern France and Montpellier before being drafted for mandatory military service. Having spent his younger years browsing through museums in Paris, the young graduate requested to serve out his public service as a 'conscientious objector' at the Musée des Arts Décoratifs, where he secured an assistant position following his release from duty. Saillard spent five years as the director of the Musée de la Mode in Marseille before returning to Paris in 2002. Serving as a fashion curator at the Parisian Musée de la Mode prior to his current appointment, Saillard staged a number of exhibitions featuring Yohji Yamamoto, Christian Lacroix and Sonia Rykiel from the museum's vast archive.

Elizabeth Semmelhack

"Fashion is central to our economic structure and it has been central to economic structures throughout time. Clothing is incredibly nuanced and discursive, and is essential to establishing everything from gender to status."[323]

Elizabeth Semmelhack has been the senior curator of the Bata Shoe Museum in Toronto since 2000. She received her M.A. in Western Art History Theory and she completed her doctorate work in Japanese Art History. Since coming to the Bata Shoe Museum, her work has focused on the construction of gender in relation to dress with a particular focus on the history of elevating footwear.

In her position, Semmelhack has curated numerous exhibitions as well as written a number of books, essays and articles. She has been the shoe consultant to the Metropolitan Museum of Art's Costume Institute, is frequent lecturer and has been widely quoted in media, such as *The New York Times*, *Wall Street Journal* and the *Washington Post*.

Kaat Debo

"Fashion is experiencing an ongoing process of democratization and you no longer have a few designers dictating what people should wear. It's much more complex than that."[324]

Kaat Debo is the director of Mode Museum (MoMu) Antwerp's fashion museum. In just over 10 years, the 37-year-old Debo has defined, more than anyone else, what exactly a fashion museum is, with successful exhibitions like the Maison Martin Margiela *20* show under her belt. With her innovative ideas and aspirational leadership, she's been able to turn MoMu into an international reference for connoisseurs of fashion.

Alexandra Palmer

"While contemporary fashion designers, such as Martin Margiela, fetishize and embrace deconstruction, museums

291

with costumes and textiles deal with this situation on a daily basis. This story of fashion is completely silenced in costume exhibitions and publications."[325]

Alexandra Palmer is the Nora E. Vaughan Fashion Costume Senior curator and chair of the Veronika Gervers Research Fellowship in Textiles & Costume at the Royal Ontario Museum (ROM) in Ontario, Canada. She's also a co-curator of BIG, the latest exhibit in the ROM's Patricia Harris Gallery of Textiles & Costume. She has been cross-appointed and teaches Fine Art History at the University of Toronto, the Graduate Programme in Art History at York University and the School of Graduate Studies at Ryerson University.

A Canadian born in Greece and raised in England, Palmer received her B.A. in Art History from the University of Toronto, her M.A. in the History of Costume & Textiles from New York University in conjunction with the Costume Institute at the Metropolitan Museum and her Ph.D. in Design History from the University of Brighton.

Before she came to the ROM in 1997, she was an assistant professor for Craft and Design History at Nova Scotia College of Art. At the ROM, she has curated *Measure for Measure* (1989) at the Samuel European Galleries, *Au Courant: Contemporary Canadian Fashion* (1997) and *Papiers à la Mode* for The Institute of Contemporary Culture (2001) as well as *Unveiling the Textiles & Costume Collection* (spring 2002), *Elite Elegance: Couture in the Feminine Fifties* (November 2002-spring 2003) and the exhibits in the Patricia Harris Gallery of Textiles & Costume since it opened in 2007.

How is curation changing the Fashion Industry?

According to Carrie Whitehead, the product and XU manager of Zappos: "If you think about it, fashion may actually be THE industry that started the curation trend – we just didn't know it at the time. How could we? 'curation' is a relatively new term, but it's finding its way into other realms; you hear about content curation, music curation – all meaning that, in some way, these industries are personalizing their offers according to your individual wants, needs and likes... Curated retail is nothing new.

Traditional brick-and-mortar stores have always relied on strategic merchandise presentation, attractive window displays and helpful sales associates to grab their customers' attentions and help them discover new products.

Although online stores may not have the advantage of this physical and in-person appeal, they are using consumer data, advanced technologies and social media to take the curated experience to the next level."[326]

Based on earlier examples of fashion curation in museums, what Whitehead said has some merit. As such, it implies that 'curation' in and of itself isn't the sole catalyst for change in the fashion industry. Rather, the marriage of curation and technology is leading the way for current and future fashion innovation.

According to LookLab founders Suraj and Radha Kapoor, "Innovative online fashion companies are causing technology and fashion to become a lot more tightly knit than they previously were. Such companies are helping deliver new levels of efficiency to their consumers, engaging them with new and innovative ideas, and providing unparalleled access to the industry."[327]

According to Nadia Buick and Madeline King, "Design curation is a growing field, with fashion, perhaps, its most popular exponent. In an era when institutions are expected to proactively engage audiences with a range of media, it makes sense that design curators are embracing the potential of the Web."[328]

Fashion Curation Takeaways

There is still space for both brick-and-mortar shops and online stores as they offer diverse experiences that are unique to each method. This simply provides myriad options for fashion-forward consumers and those individuals wanting to be on trend at all times.

Chapter 31: curation for Thought Leaders

Thought leaders are the people who make and influence the way that others see the world. They are the ones who spearhead new directions in large groups of people and are often the ones to introduce and help others embrace new concepts. They often work at or run firms that are literally the gurus within and trendsetters of their fields. Anyone called a thought leader is often expected to not only update the world on new trends, concepts and news, but also provide high-end content considered to be at the cutting edge of the industry. Curation software and content curation techniques, in general, therefore, are extremely helpful for those who are or want to be thought leaders.

How Do Thought Leaders Use Content curation?

Those who aim to be thought leaders, as well as those who actually are, can easily tell you that content is king. Content curation, therefore, is a clear must for thought leaders who want to present the very best of the net in an organized, user-friendly manner.

According to many experts, doing content curation involves more than just using curation tools to gather interesting notes from the Web. An aggregate of different snippets from the net, presented using a hub curation tool or a blog post, may get views. However, for thought leaders, this is not what content curation should be all about. Ideal content curation not only features an aggregate of posts, but also a new perspective or concept that one can derive from taking it all in.[329]

The selection of the content that thought leaders curate is also a major sticking point for those leaders who work to provide good content.

The Process of Finding Good Content as a Thought Leader

Define Your Niche

A niche market is what you need in order to break through as a thought leader. It not only helps curators focus on a topic, but also works to improve their overall abilities to search for content.

Find Content Sources and Pick Quality Content

A collection of quality, content-rich sites that are used by curators to get their content is their primary sources list. A wide selection of different sources is crucial to curation success, which is why a primary source list should be ever-expanding.

In order to get great curation, one has to pick quality posts from their sources. Low quality articles will not have the same powerful punches as good ones, so using low quality articles does not make sense. The articles need to be quality, original and relevant to your niche.

Organize and Frame

Introduce the content and add your own perspective. You want this content to be fresher than the average. After you're done framing the content in its own unique context, organize it using a nice format that is shareable to your audience. Make sure to credit your sources in order to avoid DCMA (Digital Millennium Copyright Act) write-ups or accusations of content stealing.

Framing your content means that it has to be presented in a more bite-sized and digestible manner than its raw format. Content curation tools, such as Juxtapose or Pinterest, can significantly improve user experiences.

It's crucial to remember that the format you choose will also impact your success and the choices that you make. As curator Rebecca Lieb said, "Content curation can take many forms: feeds, channels, it can appear on blogs..."[330] The format that you choose will help or harm your chances of engaging or entertaining your niche audience.[331]

Share!

Sharing your content is an important part of good curation. Use platforms that your niche is known to use and make an effort to engage the audience with your content. Tracking engagement and sharing efforts will tell you how well you've done. Your tracking work can be done through analytics programs available on content curation tool sites, such as BazaarVoice.

How Do Thought Leaders Transmit Their Curated Content?

Thought leaders already understand the importance of sharing high-end content with their targeted audiences. The ways that they transmit their curated content can make or break their campaign work and will also influence the reactions that they get. Common sense dictates the following points:

Curated content will only be read if it's being sent out on platforms that your target audience uses

Safe choices for almost any industry include Facebook, Google+, Pinterest and Twitter. Email and blogging platforms also are known to be excellent choices. More visual options include Instagram.

Different social curation tools help market content curation in a way that is understandable and appealing

Thought leaders are generally the first ones to realize the importance of aesthetics and organization in any form of curation, which is why most thought leaders will never stoop to curating "the old fashioned way" – sans add-ons and tools.

Thought leaders will often team up with other thought leaders in order to gain a wider audience

It is common knowledge that collaboration spreads awareness, publicity and influence. Thought leaders will often team up with others of equal or higher statuses for major projects. Such teamwork allows both parties to gain followers, divide the workload and spread their influence.

In some cases, such as on Facebook, thought leaders may also boost content-filled posts with paid advertising

This tactic has proven to be highly effective for many companies.

Transmitting content via email updates to mailing lists, while also promoting the content online via social media platforms is advisable

The more venues that one uses for content curation transmission, the better off you will be.

Every mode of curation transmission should be shareable

This tactic increases the power that any advertising endeavor will have.

What Experts Say About Content Curation

Content curation has definitely earned its proponents and fans throughout the Internet marketing community. Pawan Deshpande writing in *Forbes,* noted that the vast majority of Internet marketers have turned to content curation due to an increased amount of low quality postings, a growing need for social media usage, and an increased focus on building trust through good content. Deshpande mentioned that one study showed that 96% of Internet marketers have done content curation work within the past six months.[332]

Other experts, when asked about content curation, are more focused on quality and originality. Joshua Merritt strongly suggested focusing on delivering high quality content with its own unique spin. His advice includes making sure things stay relevant and immediate to the current trends and issues, and mixing aggregated content with your own, unique work.[333]

Clearly, thought leaders who want to get ahead must learn how to improve their curation efforts. It's something that experts and top leaders all agree upon.

Lee Odden, writing on the TopRank Blog, polled a number of thought leaders on how they use curation and his results were powerful and telling.[334] The results of that research follows.

Rebecca Lieb – @lieblink

Vice President of North America Econsultancy

"Content curation, which can be defined as a highly proactive and selective approach to finding, collecting, presenting and displaying digital content around predefined sets of criteria and subject matter, has become essential to marketing, branding, journalism, reporting and social media – often, to mash-ups of all these different and disparate channels.

"Content curation can takes many forms: feeds, 'channels' (such as on YouTube), it can appear on blogs, or even be the links you upload to social media sites, such as Facebook. It can be an online newsroom, a collection of links, an assortment of RSS feeds or a Twitter list. Whatever form content curation does take, it's around a topic, a subject or even a sensibility that speaks to the knowledge, expertise, taste, refinement, brand message or persona of the person, brand or company that has created the particular channel or source of content.

"Why bother? Tons of reasons. It's a big Web out there. More and more, people rely on trusted sources: friends, family, brands, companies, experts, you-name-it, to help keep them informed, educated and even amused. Need proof? Take bOINGbOING.net, one of the Web's most popular blogs whose traffic often exceeds that of the NYTimes.com. This group blog is nothing more (or less) than curated content; items its contributors and often its readers find and share with others.

"Channels of content can be as specific as beekeeping equipment or as amorphous as 'what's cool.' But they all serve multiple purposes, ranging from informing to engaging to entertaining. In an era where marketing is supplanting advertising and storytelling is an ever-more essential part of the marketing message, carefully curated content – well-presented – is an immense brand asset, be it to a humble, over-caffeinated individual blogger or a Fortune 100 company."

Ann Handley – @marketingprofs

Chief Content Officer at MarketingProfs

"Defined as it applies to online publishing, content curation is the act of continually identifying, selecting and sharing the best and most relevant online content and other online resources (and by that I mean articles, blog posts, videos, photos, tools, tweets or whatever) on a specific subject to match the needs of a specific audience.

"What role should it play:

"All organizations are now publishers — meaning the company with the most engaging and interesting content is the one who wins. Content curation isn't necessarily anything new (finding the best stuff to share is what so many of us do on Twitter already, and what bloggers have long done, or what sites like Alltop or Digg have been doing). But, recently, it's getting a little more attention as an emerging field of its own.

"It can fit into an organization's content strategy nicely. How? It's a way for organizations to further their roles as resources to their audiences. Sifting through the mountain of Web content and finding the tastiest, choicest bits for your readers is a great way to build trust and authority with them, and to become a valuable resource for them on any particular topic. What's more, for organizations just getting into publishing online — for those just starting a blog, say, or a microsite — curated content can allow them to ramp up quickly, both from an SEO as well as a content perspective.

"That said, I have two cautionary pieces of advice:

"1. Don't rely exclusively on automated content curation services to feed your own belly (to fulfill your content needs). I see content services, like HiveFire, as providing an intelligent stream of curated stuff, but you still need a real, live human Editor to pick and choose and order the best stuff for your own audience. Warm-blooded humans still required, in other words.

"2. Mix curated content with original content, and don't rely on the curated stuff alone. Content curating is a perfectly good way to extend the content of your own site, but only 'in addition to' and not 'instead of' your original content."

Joe Pulizzi – @juntajoe

Founder at Junta42 and the Content Marketing Institute; Co-Author *of Get Content, Get Customers.*

"Content curation is editing on steroids. In actuality, content curation has been around since the dawn of the publishing industry. The job of the Editor was to take the best information from around the industry and present that information in a manner that makes sense to readers.

"The Web's first crack at this was content aggregation, or having computers pull the best links and information automatically to make the 'reader's' experience more fulfilling. But, as we have learned, search is not perfect. Enter the content curation specialist.

"As more content floods through all aspects of the Web (as well as print and online), we'll need more brands stepping up to make sense of what we really should be paying attention to. Content curation is as important in the content marketing toolbox as is creation. We need both...and curation doesn't work without creation (much like Google trying to save the newspapers because they need great news to survive, but that is for another story). For some brands, curation may be enough. You can't find the resources to develop the most valuable, most compelling content in your industry? Then just tap into your network that does, and package that content to present you as the trusted industry leader. It's still a needed service, just a bit different from creation.

"Where it will go, no one knows...but I've heard from smarter people than me that content curation is the future (even present) of media. I'd rather say curation and creation go together like macaroni and cheese...a splendid combination."

Paul Gillin – @pgillin

Consultant. Author of *The New Influencers* and *Secrets of Social Media Marketing*

"I define content curation as the process of assembling, summarizing, categorizing and interpreting information from multiple sources in a context that is relevant to a particular audience. I think this discipline will be absolutely essential to content marketing in the future because of changes in the media landscape.

"Just a few years ago, audiences were starved for information and the role of media was to create it. Today, we are drowning in information and the emerging role for media is to filter and organize it.

"This is being handled accomplished on an ad hoc basis by social news sites, like Digg and Sphinn; social bookmarking sites, like Delicious and reddit; news aggregators, like Drudge Report; link blogs, like Metafilter and Slashdot; friend networks, like Twitter and Facebook; and even self-curated RSS aggregations. In fact, much of what goes on in social media [comes in] various forms of content curation.

"Marketers can build trust with their constituencies by providing focused curation in areas that matter to their constituents. Original content will always have value, but curation is coming to have nearly equal value. The key is to stake out unique topic areas and become the most trusted source in those areas. You don't need a lot of money to do this. You just need to know the subject matter very well."

Erik Qualman - @equalman

Author of *Socialnomics*, MBA. "Professor at the Hult International Business School

"Today, everyone is a potential media outlet. A curator understands [his] audience and is able to package created content in a digestible manner for [it].

"Creators need to view curators as distribution points for their content rather than as pirates. Content creators and curators [who] will thrive in this new world understand the importance of this symbiotic relationship. But is it symbiotic? In the end, almost every person is a little of both (creator and curator). After all, there is no such thing as a new idea and imitation is the sincerest form of flattery. These clichés symbolize the irony of the topic being discussed."

Valeria Maltoni – @conversationage

Director of Strategy, Powered, Inc., Conversation Agent

"Content curation is one of the keystones in a content marketing strategy. It's like museum curation — harvesting, researching, tagging, organizing and sharing — only two-way because of the digital medium. Thanks to technology it also includes in and out feeds, and moderation and escalation, where necessary.

"To maximize its impact, you want to integrate curation within a canvas of brand generated content and promotions in a forum that also highlights the best brand-related content from your own community of fans. The curator monitors conversations for opportunities to align the voice of the brand with the voice of the customer, engage outside content creators, highlight the best third-party content within the brand's sharing strategy and inspire action."

Marc Meyer – @marc_meyer

Principal and Director of Social Media and Search at DRMG

"Content today is not your father's content... Hell, it's not even the content from 10 years ago. It's so much more now. So much so, it should be its own country. Curation for us, is part art and part science. At its core, it has as much to do with maintaining and preserving what has been digitally 'created' as it does in making sure that it lasts longer than a cup of coffee. And that's the challenge.

"Loosely defined, the curation of content is a company's ability to create and then manifest digital assets that drive and maintain, at the least, awareness. Content curation, holistically speaking, refers to a person's or company's ability to stay in front of the digital curve by managing those assets across the board.

"Its role in a content marketing strategy is primary and cannot be downgraded to a perfunctory responsibility. Curation feeds the beast and, thus, contributes greatly to a company's overall digital strategy."

CURATION FOR ENTREPRENUERS

Chapter 32: Curation for Entrepreneurs

Content curation is driving more than existing businesses and marketing campaigns. Entirely new industries and movements being born around curation.

Individuals who view themselves as social activists and media-related entrepreneurs have been using content curation and creation to bring issues out of the shadows and into public view. Some of the best examples of the power of content curation include the Kony campaign, Internet feminist campaigns and the many revolutions that were sparked during the Arab Spring events.[335] This also helps build a stronger advocacy community and allows savvy curators to give the full story on their organization.

Entrepreneurs who use content curation are using it for company image management, advertising, lead generation and reputation management. In some cases, actual companies are being created that are solely focused on helping other companies establish a content curation campaign for their online businesses.[336]

The Curation Economy and the Startups It Drives

Content curation has already managed to make certain startups not only viable, but thriving businesses that have become examples of what happens when entrepreneurs harness the true power of the Internet. Many of the sectors that have been impacted by the content curation revolution have become some of the most profitable venues in recent years.

Information-Focused Startups

Startups that focus on selling classes that hone individuals' skills as well as startups that focus on information distribution have greatly benefited from having content curation drive their marketing campaigns. Social curation tools, including many of the pages of this book, have proven themselves to be excellent routes by which to gain attention from interested groups as well as routes through which to recruit experts to promote their causes and issues.

Media Startups

Much like information-focused startups, media startups have been using curation in order to amplify the amount of attention that they receive. Content curation also sparks a large amount of creativity from both fans and potential hires alike. Publishing houses and film companies have secured both investors and buyers because of curation platform participation.

Social Media Startups

Startups that yearn to become the next major social media platform are seriously impacted by content curation tools. As more and more people begin to share sites of interest as well as experiences that they have had on new social media platforms with others, social media startups are going to be forced to pay attention to their performances on these types of platforms. Social media startups not only use curation for content creation, advertising and online reputation management, but also have released their own content curation tools as products.

SEO Startups

Most businesses are not only aware of, but fully acknowledge the power of the SEO. Many startups offering SEOs and online reputation management systems have been using content curation to improve the results that their clients receive. Content curation campaign management is also a common service offered by startups in this category, which, in turn, boosts the demand for the companies' services.

Online Retailers and Affiliate Marketers

Very few online economies have been as heavily impacted as online retailers and the affiliate marketers they employ. Affiliate marketers who want to get the word out about specific products have been known to use YouTube playlists to establish a more positive reputation for the product. Amazon lists have been popular among affiliate marketers and online retailers for years. Even Pinterest has been successfully used to promote products from online retailers and affiliates alike.

Nonprofits and Those in Need of Funding

Both entrepreneurs who have a need for angel investors and nonprofit organizations known for fundraising have gotten the funds that they have needed due to the shares and promotions that they have received via content curation. It was actually social curation tools, such as Twitter, as well as more subtle curation algorithms used by social media platforms that made Zach Brown's joke "Kickstarter for Potato Salad" a viral hit. Instead of receiving a budget of $10 as he expected, Brown ended up getting over $37,000 in donations for his bowl of potato salad. While this situation is unlikely to happen to most who use curation as a way to spread the word about their causes, it does prove what can happen when curation begins to take on a life of its own.

Truth be told, almost any company or industry that relies on the Internet for lead generation will find a need to pay more attention to curation in the coming years. As Google's search engine algorithms begin to rely more and more on human factors, Internet-based entrepreneurs would be wise to cater to the more human side of the net's need for content and work harder at promoting their own curation efforts.[337]

Five curation Entrepreneurs and Startups You Should Know About

Curation has definitely become a major player in the entrepreneurial world. This has given rise to many entrepreneurs and organizations that focus on content curation as both a product and a concept. Here are five unique curation entrepreneurs and how their focus on content curation has managed to become their source of income.

SheLaunched

Sheena Miranda is the curator and CEO of SheLaunched, a startup that focuses on helping women entrepreneurs

improve their businesses and discover interesting content geared toward the struggles and challenges that women face when opening their own businesses.[338] Miranda launched this simple startup as a curated email catering to female entrepreneurs. Each email features a wide variety of different media. Links to books, videos, news articles and podcasts that have been handpicked are par for the course, and her list of signups is expanding every day.

The Entrepreneur Within

Also known as TEW, this startup is known for providing entrepreneurs with a slew of exceptional resources, including books, workshops, podcasts and even guided meet-ups geared toward networking and learning.[339] Curator and CEO Julie M. Holloway uses her passion

for the arts and business as well as her keen eye for interesting, thought-provoking content to create a collection of content that makes the average entrepreneur's eyes grow wide with interest.

TED Talks

In recent years, TED Talks have become a part of popular culture and one of the most popular sources of intellectual, curated content on the net. Oxford graduate Chris Anderson is the curator and current CEO of the TED conferences. The goal behind this startup was to

provide an outlet for people to share ideas that were unique, innovative and "worth spreading."[340] Since the first TED conference in the mid-80s, this channel of content has become a pop culture phenomenon, created an extremely popular YouTube channel and boosted several educators to national fame.

STLcurator

A team of entrepreneurs and writers spearheaded STLcurator, a startup devoted to bringing the good side of St. Louis to the forefront. [341]

Their content focuses on taking attention away from the

crime stories that are constantly being featured in the national news and showing the city as a booming, friendly area that actually has a lot of potential to become a major cultural center and haven for entrepreneurs. Though brand new, the site has received a lot of positive press.

Venture Hacks

Babak Nivi and Naval Ravikant are the dynamic duo behind Venture Hacks and AngelList, two major sites geared toward aiding startups make it big.[342] Venture Hacks is a curated content site in the form of a blog that focuses on providing valuable information, news and advice to those individuals new to the business world. AngelList, on  the other hand, is a site that works to connect entrepreneurs with investors, other startups and other technology that improves their abilities to turn a profit. AngelList has not only helped major startups get the money they needed to become real, but also has managed to turn a staggering profit within a matter of years.

Part 6

Ready. Set. Curate.

Chapter 33: What Comes Next? The Digital Desert Island

W ell now, you've gotten to the end of the book. Congratulations. Ok, you skipped a few chapters, that's fine, and you probably didn't agree with everything that you've read. That's fine, too. However, - here's the big surprise, chances are, - you've come to a conclusion that is 100% wrong.

For many folks, there's an assumption that the Web and the world will continue down the path they are on; that the noise will continue to become increasingly overwhelming and that the volume of tweets, posts and links will continue to expand. Do you believe that the overwhelming avalanche of content will continue? If you believe that, you're not alone. But that future is simply not possible.

Why? Because humans need sleep. We need down time. We need the sun on our faces, the wind in our hair, the sound of wind chimes and moments of solitude and peace.

So, - if you've have been thinking of about curation as another tool in your arsenal to win the arms race of content creation, then you've got it all wrong.

Sure, you can use curation to generate thousands of related content links and, you can out-shout your competition. You can tweet more than others in your space, and retweet with abandon..... And that will work, until, like a light switch, it doesn't. Then, at that moment, you will have lost the trust of your audience and your followers. And you've lost them forever.

So, before you use curation to further destroy the Web environment we so count on to power our information ecology, I'd like to propose an alternative approach; A big idea, with a remarkable outcome. Remember that, with great power comes great responsibility, and curation - properly used - is certainly a great power.

Here's a view of the future that you haven't considered, and a solution that makes the world and your role in it better.

The Digital Desert Island

Today, sites and content creators are all working tirelessly to make the world of the future look like the world of the past. Advertisers think wistfully about the time, not so long ago, when you could buy big swaths of the population with a stroke of a pen. Mass media was efficient, effective and measurable. If you had the budget, you could own your audience. It was for a rare moment, an advertiser's dream come true. With limited access to television and radio airwaves, and costly printing presses, the media was powerful and advertising inventory scarce.

Then, the walls came down. First with cable television and then with the Internet; the scarcity of distribution was replaced with abundance. The democratization of publishing technology turned everyone into bloggers, first with platforms like WordPress and Blogger.com, and then, as the volume of information grew, with the emergence of microblogging with Tumblr, Twitter and Facebook. The result was an arms race of information turning the formerly alluring Web into an exhausting endless journey into random and unrelated bits of information. At the same time, advertisers who were unable to find the technology necessary to deliver the holy grail of media buying (i.e., identifiable and appropriately targetable audiences) instead reverted to the mass media model of rewarding sites able to reach large audiences. Mass media dollars began chasing the Web's natural evolution toward narrowcast niche media.

So, as this book began, I once again state what we now all know, we broke the Web. However, the trend toward the random avalanche of information won't go on forever. In fact, it's about to end. We are all just a click away from building our own Digital Desert Island.

How does this sound. You live on an island. Around you is an ocean that spammers, marketers and even your friends and family can't broach to get to you - without your permission. On your island, you have peace. Your family is invited. Your close friends are invited. A few media sources with whom you've shared your trusted space are invited. You've also invited some social networks as they have given you the tools needed to honestly focus and filter who reaches you and how they are to reach you. There are even some brands that you trust that have been invited, but they too must respect your interests in regard to the way in which you want to hear from them and how you communicate with them. You control who's invited to your island and you can rescind that permission at any time.

The idea of permission isn't new. My friend, Seth Godin, understood the future when he coined the phrase 'Permission Marketing' in 1999.[343] However, as right as Godin was, the temptation to carpet bomb the Web with spam-like advertising proved too alluring. Until now, brands, media companies and publishers could afford to pollute the Web with an ever growing spam-like stream of mostly irrelevant information.

However, once consumers have the tools and filters to build their own Digital Desert Islands everything will change in an instant. Just to be clear, there's nothing particularly hard about giving consumers filters and barriers. On the distribution side, there's little incentive to do that. Twitter, Facebook and LinkedIn are all rewarded handsomely for growing their scale. Ad agencies are paid to gather and distribute impressions, and brands reward media buying companies for reaching audience at scale.

So, until the tools arrive, the entire information ecology will remain polluted and brands, media companies and content creators will be rewarded for creating noise, not signal.

However, the tools are about to arrive. In fact, I can share with you the very first example of a Digital Desert Island tool that I have added to my self-defense kit. It's called The Black Hole. If you email me, a service called Sane Box separates emails from my friends and co-workers into one folder called "Sane Now" and all of my other email into the folder labeled "Sane Later." While this service is similar to the Priority Inbox provided by Gmail, it goes one step further and gives me a folder called "Black Hole."

For marketers who disrespect my time, all it takes is a click... and they're gone. Radio Shack and Best Buy both crossed the line for me. Too many emails, too much noise, not enough signal. They tried to sell me products that I didn't need and they didn't respect my time. So, they're both in the black hole. The thing is I didn't click 'unsubscribe.' They're still delivering their messages to me, but thanks to Sane Box, I never see them. These brands think that they're still reaching me, but they're not. Sadly, since I wasn't given the tools to teach the brands my interests (i.e., Radio Shack: I like Arduino and radio controlled helicopters, but don't need to ever hear about Bluetooth speakers), I've simply tuned them out.

Tuning Out. Tuning In.

This is why curation is critically important. It's not so that you can out-shout, out-tweet and out-blog your competition. To use content as an offensive weapon is to declare war on your most critical asset, your audience.

The question today is - if your customer had a Digital Desert Island that he could live on, would he invite you to join him? Would your curation be thoughtful, relevant and contextual? Is your curatorial voice making the Web a clearer, smarter and more human scaled place?

In wrapping up this book, I wanted to take a moment to give you some helpful guidelines on how curation can prepare you for the future and how, if misused, it can hasten your demise.

Five curation Rules to Live By:

- Listen to Your Audience

  Tweet Less, Not More

- Video Matters - More than You Think

- curation is a Two-way Street

- In the Future, Your Customers Will Filter the Fire hose

Listening

Listening is more than having an intern read hashtags in a Twitter stream. Listening means actively creating an environment in which your fans, customers and friends are invited to engage in a conversation with you. It means asking questions, inviting feedback and respecting the fact that some of that feedback will be critical, even painful. Brands that survive in the new world of the Digital Desert Island won't simply write off criticism or try to stifle dialog. Opening yourself up to dialog is critical to harnessing the power of the Web. Can you imagine tweeting "What Can We Do Better #learningfromyou"? If you can't imagine that - ask yourself why? In the olden days, customers filled out comment cards. The feedback was compiled by customer service and read by executives (maybe), but it remained private.

Today, unhappy customers have access to your brand. They can tweet, post on Facebook or create a YouTube video, Vine or Instagram. Salacious and snarky posts are going to get shared, so, chances are that if you don't give your customers a forum for feedback and conversation, they're going to find one on their own.

On the other hand, brands, media companies and services that activate their users have a powerful new resource.

Curating the conversation can create an energy that is positive, open and empowering. Either way, the horse is out of the barn. The days of one-way control are over.

Less is more

On the Digital Desert Island, customers value lean, clean communication. They value solitude. They value relevance. Trying to out-yell your competition or the cacophony of the Web is an effort that's doomed to fail. On the other hand, creating crisp, tight, curated voices is a powerful solution. Imagine that you're an ecommerce company, not sending out a 50 page printed catalog or its digital equivalent. Instead, you give your visitors their choice of topic-specific Editorial and product experiences.

Imagine a mix of news, stories, pictures, video and ecommerce that delights your customers. It mixes edit and commerce with style and crisp curatorial vision. It even has room for user-contributed content where your customers share their experiences and love of your style. All of a sudden, as a reader, I'm getting just what interests me. Ok, I know you're saying, "but you need to share things to customers who don't know what they want." In the old world, you could overwhelm them with page after page of uninvited goods and services, but, in the new world, where time is scarce and content is abundant, the best value you can provide is tightly curated experiences. If you earn your customers' trust and respect their precious time, then you can offer an opportunity to explore other categories and related offerings...but not before they trust you.

Video matters, more than you think

Since TV was invented, it's been about reaching the largest audience with the most broadly appealing content. However, Web video isn't old-time TV. It's a whole new thing. It's curated TV and that means its mission is no longer to 'go viral' or reach the largest audience. Video, for the emerging mobile audience, is a two-way street. It's created, shared, re-mixed and explored in new way. If you're not telling your story with video, then you're missing a medium that a generation of consumers thinks of as its primary source of communication. Video curation is a place where you've got a powerful potential to give your customers an important and unique service. Video, unlike text, is hard to scan and hard to search. YouTube and search broadly tends to default to video that is the most popular, but popularity is a terrible measure of relevance or value.

Imagine for a moment that you're a cruise line. Every one of your customers has a cell phone with an HD video recorder built in. Chances are, all of your customers shoot video. Some share tips and tricks about great cruise experiences. Others record a few minor quibbles with the service. Of that video, 99% remains on the phones or is shared on Facebook among friends. However, if one of your customers has a bad experience, even a minor one, then that video will go viral. Are you inviting your customers to share their stories about your products with you so that you can curate the content and publish a deep, rich collection of video that is authentic and relevant? To not embrace video is to let only the salacious or negative video float to the top. This tactic is an easy win and essential for any brand that wants to be at the center of the conversation created by its customers.

Curation is a Two-way Street

So, you're making content and you're curating content. The big question is - are you inviting others to share your content at places other than your site? Have you turned on embedding, tweeting, Facebook Posts, Google+ and more? I get it. Sharing is scary. What if a competitor grabs your content and posts it on his site? What if it ends up in places you don't want it to go? Sorry, that ship has sailed. Sharing is binary. Either you share or you don't. Imagine telling your child to take a plate of brownies to share with the class, except for Billy, none for him. The truth is that, if you've ever looked at all of the places where your content is embedded, then you're probably as baffled as I am. Blogs you've never heard of with context that seems irrelevant to you, maybe even objectionable, have embedded your posts. However, that's the nature of sharing and you're not asking permission to curate content on your site, so you can't expect the same to go in the other direction.

Chapter 34: Curate or Die

It wasn't that long ago that the word curate didn't have an application on the Web. In 2008, I began talking about how our company gathered, organized and presented content. I said we were curating content and, almost from that moment on, I was the subject of arrows and brickbats. Curators said that I had stolen their word. Editors said that curation was just editing and film and print Editors aligned to call me out for hijacking their word. However, even as the complaints and cries of hijacking a word continued to grow, something funny happened: people began to call themselves curators. Sites like *The Huffington Post* started to curate content at scale and everyone from cab drivers to school teachers found that they almost couldn't put down their phones or look away from their screens.

The content explosion put all of us in the line of fire and no longer was curation something we could simply ignore. As individuals, we're desperate for it. As marketers, we're trying to harness it. As brands, we're trying to respect it. It seems like things will just get more overwhelming until they can't get any worse. Then, like a light switch, it will change. Trust me, you want to be on the right side of that change. How do I know? Because you've been reading this book and you've made it to the end.

For some time now, the hot new buzzword for Web services has been "curation." Whether it's Pinterest, Tumblr, Flipboard or News.me, everyone wants to ride the curation wave, but what does it mean and how do you do it properly? What makes it different from aggregation? These types of debates have been around in one form or another since the Internet was invented, but have resurfaced lately thanks to two proposals. One is trying to come up with a code of conduct for curators and aggregators, and the other is promoting the use of special symbols to give credit to original sources. These efforts may be well-intentioned, but they are also misguided and likely doomed, as virtually every attempt to control the Internet has been."[344]

Respect the Role of the Curator

Do you have a business card that says "curator" on it yet? If not, chances are that you will. If it's not on your card, it will be on the card of someone you work with. So buckle up, the war for curatorial talent is just beginning.[345] "What we are seeing is the start of a war for curatorial talent. With Ebay and Amazon having made acquisitions in the curation space, and the explosive growth of Pinterest, the value of curation isn't secret anymore."[346]

The clear message of these pages, of my work, and of the technology that I have nurtured and helped bring to life is this: the world needs human scale and Editorially flexible curation. We need it urgently. We need it now. We need it to keep the avalanche of the Web's raw data from overwhelming our senses and our sanity. Most importantly, we need it because the value of the Web isn't yet fully developed and we're at a critical crossroads. Either the Web will overwhelm us and we'll simply revert to mass media and big branded media conglomerates or curation will give individuals the power to find the signal in the noise.

Curation is the thing that makes big data human scaled.

Curation is the thing that humanizes information that is created at an inhuman scale.

Curation is the place where the complexity and wonder of individuals makes us feel connected to others in our tribes.

So – go forth and curate! It's what we were built to do.

Chapter 35: A Personal Note

I've been a maker. I've been a curator. And the truth is, I love both.

As a filmmaker, writer, blogger, and photographer – I love the effort and intellectual beads of sweat that form as I have to turn ideas into something tangible.

As a curator, I feel deeply engaged in the deep end of the content pool. Finding, sharing, linking, and enhancing ideas that matter. I have Twitter followers, but I'm always happy to have more.

If you enjoyed this book, and think there's more to explore – follow me at @Waaywire on Twitter.

Or – if you want to dig deeper – hit me up on LinkedIn, Facebook, or Twitter. I'm pretty good at responding – since one-on-one is often the most effective way to turn ideas into action.

And – I am also a fan of real world engagements. So don't be shy if you are hosting an event, or looking for a speaker at your company event or conference. I host the New York Video Meetup every month, and love playing ringmaster to an energized and passionate group of innovators.

There only one way to say it. I wrote this book to meet you.
So, if you're reading this page – then this is the beginning.

And go to <u>www.CurateThisBook.com</u> to find extras.

CREDITS and APPRECIATION

Cover Design:	Nathan Lord
Researchers:	Evelyn Panagapko Ossiana Tepfenhart Nikki Forston Tracee Loran
Editors:	Emily Heinlen Davis Eileen Landay
Publication Formatting:	Amy Himebaugh
Editorial Guidance and Support:	Pamela Yoder
Website Design:	Claudia Mei Prith Pal
Public Relations & Marketing:	Biancia Francis
Literary Agent:	John Wright
My Favorite curators:	The Team at Waywire.com
Speaking Agent, Stern Speakers Bureau	Mel Blake
Special Thanks:	Guy Kawasaki, Shawn Welch "APE: How to Publish a Book"
	Niina Pollari – Kickstarter

Kickstarter Backers:

Albert Chu
Aleha
Alex Apollonsky
André Faria Gomes
Ari J. Greenberg
Arthur Mitchell
Beth Surmont
Beth Temple
Biancia Francis
Bill Bragin
Billy Linker
Brad Dickey
Brendan Cahill
Brian Abent
Bruce Frishkoff
Carla Graubard
Chad Herzog
Chaim Haas
Chris Dorr
Christopher Conetta
Clay Shirky
Clifford Bor
Cory Treffileti
Dan Murray
Daphne Kwon
David Adams
David S. Rose
Dorian Benkoil
Dot McMahon
Douglas Warshaw
Dror Shimshowitz
Dudu Torres

Edward Chik
Edward Hoover
Eileen Landay
Elena Gerstmann
Erik
Frank Barbieri
Fredric Helgesson
Hugh Forrest
Ian Isanberg
IEEE
Isabel
Janice Erlbaum
Jason Hirschhorn
JC Cangilla
JD Lasica
Jennifer Tribe
Jeremy Straight
Joel Zaslofsky
Joeseph Simon
John May
Jose Ortiz Jr
Jose Peleteiro
joshua prager
Karen Barney
Karl Jahn
Larry Boyer
LarryBud Meyer
Laurel Touby
Lee-Sean Huang
Leonieke LeoLoves
Letitia Splain Dayer
Linda Holliday

Marc Scarpa
Mark Rybarczyk
Marty Isaac
Mathew Tombers
Maurice Smith
Michael E. Meyers
Michael Moretti
MicoyGordie
Mohan Narendran
Pam Yoder
Paul E. Walsh
Paul Fish
Pawan Deshpande
Peter Kirwan
Rahlyn
Rasiej
Rick Smolan
Rodger Wells
Roger Wyatt
Sarah Knapp
Scott Hoffman
Sean Casey
Shawn Tierney
Shay Brog
Sigrid Peterson
Sjoerd Adding
Steven Strauss
Susan Gauthier
Tobin trevarthen
VivekSingh

INDEX

BIBLIOGRAPHY

[1] http://www.forbes.com/sites/stevenrosenbaum/2012/11/26/humans-vs-robots-whos-on-top

[2] http://techcrunch.com/2010/08/04/schmidt-data/

[3] http://en.wikipedia.org/wiki/Technological_singularity

[4] http://www.forbes.com/sites/stevenrosenbaum/2012/11/26/humans-vs-robots-whos-on-top/

[5] http://gigaom.com/2012/11/29/techmeme-founder-give-me-human-Editors-and-the-new-york-times

[6] http://gigaom.com/2012/11/29/techmeme-founder-give-me-human-Editors-and-the-new-york-times/

[7] http://www.siliconvalleywatcher.com/mt/archives/2010/11/curation_and_th.php

[8] http://gigaom.com/2012/11/29/techmeme-founder-give-me-human-Editors-and-the-new-york-times/

[9] http://www.businessinsider.com/narrative-science-quill-gamechanger-2014-7

[10] http://www.slate.com/articles/technology/future_tense/2012/03/narrative_science_robot_journalists_customized_news_and_the_danger_to_civil_discourse_.html

[11] http://mashable.com/2012/12/13/infographic-Native-advertising/

[12] tp://contently.com/strategist/2014/01/21/ads-that-can-compete-with-the-best-material-out-there-an-interview-with-jay-rosen-on-the-future-of-sponsored-content/

[13] http://www.forbes.com/sites/stevenrosenbaum/2012/04/10/ibm-communication-and-curation-go-hand-in-hand/

[14] http://www.forbes.com/sites/stevenrosenbaum/2012/04/10/ibm-communication-and-curation-go-hand-in-hand/

[15] http://en.wikipedia.org/wiki/Smarter_Planet

[16] http://digiday.com/publishers/ge-getting-online-news-publishing/?utm_content=buffer83bcb&utm_medium=social&utm_source=Twitter.com&utm_campaign=buffer

[17] http://digiday.com/publishers/ge-getting-online-news-publishing/?utm_content=buffer83bcb&utm_medium=social&utm_source=Twitter.com&utm_campaign=buffer

[18] http://www.mediabistro.com/prnewser/toms-chief-digital-officer-outlines-brands-giving-formula_b95783

[19] http://www.mediabistro.com/prnewser/toms-chief-digital-officer-outlines-brands-giving-formula_b95783

[20] http://www.theguardian.com/advertisingsummit/how-content-Curators-are-connecting-consumers-say-media

[21] http://www.cmo.com/articles/2014/2/24/_5_companies_that_took.html

[22] "Going Local" http://www.economist.com/node/18956576 (*The Economist*, July 14, 2011)

[23] Ibid.

[24] David Dean; Sebastain DeGrande; Dominic Field; Andreas Lundmark; James O'Day; John Pineda; Paul Zwillenberg "The Internet Economy in the G-20" https://www.bcgperspectives.com/content/articles/media_entertainment_strategic_planning_4_2_trillion_opportunity_Internet_economy_g20/ (BCG Perspectives, March 19, 2012)

[25] http://www.businessdictionary.com/definition/glocalization.html

[26] Keith Richburg "What is the Future of Local?" http://www.keithrichburg.com/blogs/keith-b-richburg/what-future-local (Keith Richburg, June 18, 2013)

[27] Ibid.

[28] Ibid.

29 Brian Womack & Alan Levin "Google Experiments Challenge Amazon" *The Philadelphia Inquirer* August 30, 2014

30 Ibid.

31 Brian Solis "Going Global By Going Local" http://www.briansolis.com/2012/01/digital-localization-optimizes-global-strategies-to-improve-experiences-and-results/ (Brian Solis, January 3, 2012)

32 Ibid.

33 Ibid.

34 Rachel Priest "Hyperlocal Content: The Future of Online Marketing?" http://www.interactmedia.com/content-marketing-blog/bid/79403/Hyperlocal-Content-The-Future-Of-Online-Marketing (Interactmedia.com, October 12, 2012)

35 Ibid.

36 Natalie Burg "Why Did Patch Dry Up: Is Hyperlocal Over or Was It AOL?" http://contently.com/strategist/2014/02/07/why-patch-dried-up-is-hyperlocal-over-or-was-it-aol/ (Contently, February 7, 2014)

37 John Moulding "Original and Local Content at the Heart of Future Netflix Strategy" http://www.v-net.tv/original-and-local-content-at-heart-of-future-netflix-strategy (Connected TV, July 23, 2014)

38 Ibid.

39 Ibid.

40 http://moz.com/blog/why-local-business-dont-need-big-budgets-for-their-content-marketing

41 http://www.toprankblog.com/2011/02/small-business-content-marketing

42 http://www.branded3.com/blogs/small-brands-can-create-big-content/

43 http://www.sitemagazine.com/content/blogs/posts/archive/2014/08/05/advantages-of-big-brand-seo-vs-small-business-seo.aspx Accessed 01/09/14

44 http://www.convinceandconvert.com/content-marketing/6-reasons-to-make-your-big-idea-small/

45 http://feldmancreative.com/2014/05/big-content-marketing-tips-small-businesses/

46 http://www.fastcompany.com/1741534/why-Curator-isnt-Editor

47 http://www.contentcurationmarketing.com/content-curation-copyright-ethics-fair-use/

48 http://journal.transformativeworks.org/index.php/twc/article/view/489/411

49 http://www.forbes.com/sites/stevenrosenbaum/2012/10/11/youtubes-curation-vision-the-impact/

50 http://tedxtalks.ted.com/video/Making-Copyright-Your-Friend-2;search%3AAufderheide

51 http://www.cmsimpact.org/fair-use/related-materials/codes/code-best-practices-fair-use-online-video

52 Scanlon, S. (2014). *Does Content Creation Help Your SEO?* Retrieved from http://curationtraffic.com/curation-tips/does-curation-help-seo/

53 DeMers, J. (2014). *6 Facts About Content Curation and SEO You May Not Know.* Retrieved from http://blog.scoop.it/2014/03/11/6-facts-about-content-curation-and-seo-you-may-not-know/

54 Fiorelli, G. (2012). *Content Curation Guide For SEO – What, How, Why.* Retrieved from http://moz.com/blog/content-curation-guide-for-seo

55 DeMers, J. (2014). *6 Facts About Content Curation and SEO You May Not Know.* Retrieved from http://blog.scoop.it/2014/03/11/6-facts-about-content-curation-and-seo-you-may-not-know/

56 DeMers, J. (2014). *Your Guide to Content Curation For SEO.* Retrieved http://www.searchenginejournal.com/guide-content-curation-seo/80773/

57 DeMers, J. (2014). *6 Facts About Content Curation and SEO You May Not Know.* Retrieved from http://blog.scoop.it/2014/03/11/6-facts-about-content-curation-and-seo-you-may-not-know/

58 DeMers, J. (2014). *6 Facts About Content Curation and SEO You May Not Know.* Retrieved from http://blog.scoop.it/2014/03/11/6-facts-about-content-curation-and-seo-you-may-not-know/

59 DeMers, J. (2014). *6 Facts About Content Curation and SEO You May Not Know.* Retrieved from http://blog.scoop.it/2014/03/11/6-facts-about-content-curation-and-seo-you-may-not-know/

60 DeMers, J. (2014). *6 Facts About Content Curation and SEO You May Not Know.* Retrieved from http://blog.scoop.it/2014/03/11/6-facts-about-content-curation-and-seo-you-may-not-know/

61 Enge, E. (2014). *Content Curation & SEO: A Bad Match?* Retrieved from http://searchenginewatch.com/article/2290885/Content-Curation-SEO-A-Bad-Match

62 DeMers, J. (2014). *6 Facts About Content Curation and SEO You May Not Know.* Retrieved from http://blog.scoop.it/2014/03/11/6-facts-about-content-curation-and-seo-you-may-not-know/

63 DeMers, J. (2014). *6 Facts About Content Curation and SEO You May Not Know.* Retrieved from http://blog.scoop.it/2014/03/11/6-facts-about-content-curation-and-seo-you-may-not-know/

64 Sutton, M. (2014). *Content Curation & SEO: Do's and Don'ts.* Retrieved from http://www.curata.com/blog/content-curation-seo-dos-and-donts/

65 http://jwikert.typepad.com/the_average_joe/2014/04/community-curation.html

66 http://colin.io/portfolio/curation-is-creation/

67 http://www.forbes.com/sites/avaseave/2014/01/29/unlocking-curation-data-drives-content-first-community/

68 https://www.techdirt.com/articles/20100215/0036438160.shtml

69 https://www.techdirt.com/articles/20100215/0036438160.shtml

70 https://www.techdirt.com/articles/20100215/0036438160.shtml

71 http://heidicohen.com/content-curation-giants-google-versus-amazon/

72 http://heidicohen.com/content-curation-giants-google-versus-amazon/

73 http://heidicohen.com/content-curation-giants-google-versus-amazon/

74 http://www.digitalpulse.pwc.com.au/content-marketing-context-curation-customisation/

75 http://www.digitalpulse.pwc.com.au/content-marketing-context-curation-customisation/

76 http://www.digitalpulse.pwc.com.au/content-marketing-context-curation-customisation/

77 http://www.digitalpulse.pwc.com.au/social-shopping-online-retailing/

78 http://www.digitalpulse.pwc.com.au/content-marketing-context-curation-customisation/

79 https://www.techdirt.com/articles/20100215/0036438160.shtml

80 http://www.digitalpulse.pwc.com.au/content-marketing-context-curation-customisation/

81 http://www.digitalpulse.pwc.com.au/content-marketing-context-curation-customisation/

82 http://heidicohen.com/content-curation-giants-google-versus-amazon/

83 http://heidicohen.com/content-curation-giants-google-versus-amazon/

84 http://www.orbitmedia.com/blog/content-curation/

85 http://www.orbitmedia.com/blog/content-curation/

86 http://www.orbitmedia.com/blog/content-curation/

87 http://www.orbitmedia.com/blog/content-curation/

88 http://curationtraffic.com/content-curation-commentary/if-you-want-to-profit-with-content-curation-you-must-own-the-platform/

89 http://www.businessweek.com/magazine/content/11_17/b4225060960537.htm

90 http://curationtraffic.com/content-curation-commentary/if-you-want-to-profit-with-content-curation-you-must-own-the-platform/

91 http://www.quora.com/What-are-the-3-best-strategies-for-monetizing-a-content-curation-site

92 http://www.shoutmeloud.com/make-money-from-content-curation.html

93http://mashable.com/2012/04/27/tips-great-content-curation/

94 http://en.wikipedia.org/wiki/Jonah_Peretti

95 http://www.wired.co.uk/magazine/archive/2014/02/features/buzzfeed

96 http://pando.com/2012/09/19/peretti-human-curation-beats-seo-in-the-social-Web/

97 http://www.buzzfeed.com/about

98 Christine Lagorio-Chafkin; "The Humble Origins of BuzzFeed" http://www.inc.com/christine-lagorio/humble-origins-of-buzzfeed.html (*Inc.*, March 3, 2014)

99 http://www.buzzfeed.com/community/about

100 David Rowan, "How BuzzFeed Mastered Social Sharing to Become a Media Giant for a New Era" http://www.wired.co.uk/magazine/archive/2014/02/features/buzzfeed (*Wired*, UK, January 2, 2014)

101 Heidi Moore, "BuzzFeed CEO Jonah Peretti Wants to Create Another Mad Men Age of Advertising" http://www.businessinsider.com/buzzfeed-and-advertorial-strategy-2013-1#ixzz2H1Vt68pZ (*Business Insider*, January 3, 2013)

102 David Rowan, "How BuzzFeed Mastered Social Sharing to Become a Media Giant for a New Era" http://www.wired.co.uk/magazine/archive/2014/02/features/buzzfeed (*Wired*, UK, January 2, 2014)

103 Ibid.

104 Ibid.

105 Mike Isaac, "50 Million New Reasons BuzzFeed Wants to Take Its Content Far Beyond Lists" http://www.nytimes.com/2014/08/11/technology/a-move-to-go-beyond-lists-for-content-at-buzzfeed.html?_r=0 (*The New York Times*, August 10, 2014)

106 Ibid.

107 Dan Frommer, "Here's How BuzzFeed Works" http://www.businessinsider.com/heres-how-buzzfeed-works-2010-6 (Business Insider, June 11, 2010)

108 Ibid.

109 Ibid.

110 David Rowan, "How BuzzFeed Mastered Social Sharing to Become a Media Giant for a New Era" http://www.wired.co.uk/magazine/archive/2014/02/features/buzzfeed (*Wired*, UK, January 2, 2014)

111 http://www.buzzfeed.com

112 Zach Schonfeld "BuzzFeed Records Your Personal Quiz Data in Bulk" http://www.newsweek.com/does-buzzfeed-know-which-backstreet-boy-you-should-actually-marry-256280 (*Newsweek*, June 25, 2014)

113 Ibid.

114 Ibid.

115 Mike Isaac, "50 Million New Reasons BuzzFeed Wants to Take Its Content Far Beyond Lists" http://www.nytimes.com/2014/08/11/technology/a-move-to-go-beyond-lists-for-content-at-buzzfeed.html?_r=0 (*The New York Times*, August 10, 2014)

116 David Rowan "How BuzzFeed Mastered Social Sharing to Become a Media Giant For a New Era" http://www.wired.co.uk/magazine/archive/2014/02/features/buzzfeed (*Wired*, UK, January 2, 2014)

117 Claire Cain Miller, "Why BuzzFeed is Trying to Shift Its Strategy" http://www.nytimes.com/2014/08/13/upshot/why-buzzfeed-is-trying-to-shift-its-strategy.html?_r=1&abt=0002&abg=1 (*The New York Times*, August 10, 2014)

118 Kelly McBride "BuzzFeed Reporter's Use of Tweets Stirs Controversy" http://www.poynter.org/latest-news/creating-a-framework-for-ethical-decision-making-

among-journalists-and-those-who-care-about-democracy/243413/buzzfeed-reporters-use-of-tweets-stirs-controversy/ (Poynter.org, March 14, 2014)

[119] Mike Isaac "50 Million New Reasons BuzzFeed Wants to Take Its Content Far Beyond Lists" http://www.nytimes.com/2014/08/11/technology/a-move-to-go-beyond-lists-for-content-at-buzzfeed.html?_r=0 (*New York Times*, August 10, 2014)

[120] Kate Magee "BuzzFeed Outlines Expansion Plans After Raising 50m" http://www.mediaweek.co.uk/article/1307531/buzzfeed-outlines-expansion-plans-raising-50m (*Media Week*, UK, August 12, 2014)

[121] Hadas Gold, "BuzzFeed's Growing Pains" http://www.politico.com/blogs/media/2014/08/buzzfeeds-growing-pains-194121.html (*Politico*, August 18, 2014)

[122] Ibid.

[123] David Rowan "How BuzzFeed Mastered Social Sharing to Become a Media Giant for a New Era" http://www.wired.co.uk/magazine/archive/2014/02/features/buzzfeed (*Wired*, UK, January 2, 2014)

[124] http://pando.com/2012/09/19/peretti-human-curation-beats-seo-in-the-social-Web/

[125] http://www.adweek.com/news/technology/fast-company-declares-upworthy-fastest-growing-media-site-all-time-150195

[126] http://www.businessinsider.com/upworthy-how-to-create-a-fast-growing-media-company-2012-11?op=1

[127] http://blog.upworthy.com/post/88657827841/the-most-weve-ever-said-about-curation-at-upworthy
http://www.slideshare.net/Upworthy/how-to-make-that-one-thing-go-viral-just-kidding

[128] http://www.nj.com/news/index.ssf/2012/07/newark_mayor_cory_booker_plans.html

[129] http://www.nj.com/news/index.ssf/2012/06/booker_helps_launch_social_med.html

[130] http://amix.dk/blog/post/19588

[131] http://www.reddit.com/wiki/faq

[132] http://www.prdaily.com/Main/Articles/5_reddit_tips_for_brand_managers_14860.aspx

[133] https://www.tumblr.com/about

[134] Doug Aamoth "What is Tumblr" http://techland.time.com/2013/05/19/what-is-tumblr/ (*Time*, May 19, 2013)

[135] http://en.wikipedia.org/wiki/UrbanBaby

[136] Jenna Wortham, Nick Bilton "Before Tumblr, Founder Made Mom Proud. He Quit School" http://www.nytimes.com/2013/05/21/technology/david-karp-quit-school-to-get-serious-about-startups.html?pagewanted=all&_r=0 (*New York Times*, May 20, 2013)

[137] Liz Welch "David Karp, the Nonconformist Who Built Tumblr" http://www.inc.com/magazine/201106/the-way-i-work-david-karp-of-tumblr.html (*Inc.*, June 2011)

[138] Ibid.

[139] Ibid.

[140] Ibid.

[141] Chris Isidore "Yahoo Buys Tumblr, Promises Not to 'Screw It Up'" http://money.cnn.com/2013/05/20/technology/yahoo-buys-tumblr/ (CNN Money, May 20, 2013)

[142] Christine Erikson "The Beginner's Guide to Tumblr" http://mashable.com/2012/06/03/the-beginners-guide-to-tumblr/ (Mashable, June 3, 2012)

[143] Ibid.

[144] John McDermott http://digiday.com/platforms/apple-chose-tumblr-social-media-debut/ (Digiday, March 4, 2014)

[145] Nate Smitha "Should Tumblr Be Part of Your Social Strategy?" http://simplymeasured.com/blog/2013/08/29/should-tumblr-be-a-part-of-your-social-strategy/ (Simply Measured, August 29, 2013)
[146] Albert Costill "50 Things You Should Know About Tumblr" http://www.searchenginejournal.com/50-things-know-tumblr/84595/ (Search Engine Journal, January 9, 2014)
[147] Ibid.
[148] Ibid.
[149] Matt Brian "Tumblr iOS app Updated With Twitter and Facebook Sharing" http://www.theverge.com/2013/4/24/4260392/tumblr-ios-update-adds-facebook-Twitter-sharing
[150] Albert Costill "50 Things You Should Know About Tumblr" http://www.searchenginejournal.com/50-things-know-tumblr/84595/ (Search Engine Journal, January 9, 2014)
[151] Ibid.
[152] Ibid.
[153] Dan Schawbel "David Karp on Tumblr's Growth, Monetization and Future Plans" http://www.forbes.com/sites/danschawbel/2013/01/02/david-karp-on-tumblrs-growth-monetization-mentors-and-future-plans/ (Forbes, January 2, 2013)
[154] http://www.ignitesocialmedia.com/blogging/4-tips-for-brand-marketing-success-on-tumblr/
[155] http://www.shoutlet.com/blog/2013/03/sxsw-takeaway-round-up-part-2-the-future-is-personalized/
[156] http://brands.tumblr.com/start
[157] Nicholas Carlson "Pinterest CEO: Here's How We Became the Web's Next Big Thing" http://www.businessinsider.com/pinterest-founding-story-2012-4?op=1 (Business Insider, April 24, 2012)
[158] Ibid.
[159] Ibid.
[160] Ibid.
[161] Ibid.
[162] Haley Hinseth "The History of Pinterest" http://thehistoryofpinterest.blogspot.com (Weblog)
[163] Jennifer Marshall "Experian Marketing Services Pinpoints Rising Social Network Sites in New Study - Instagram and Pinterest Lead the Pack" http://www.experian.com/blogs/news/2012/08/11/instagram-pinteres/ (Experian News Blog, August 11, 2012)
[164] Matt Kapko "Pinterest Pins Revenue Plans on Ad Targeting" http://www.cio.com/article/2375860/social-media/pinterest-pins-revenue-plans-on-ad-targeting.html (CIO, May 30, 2014)
[165] "Pinterest 101: Getting Started With Pinterest" http://www.gcflearnfree.org/pinterest101/2 (GCF LearnFree.org)
[166] Ibid.
[167] Erica Ayotte "What the Heck is Pinterest and Why Should You Care?" http://blogs.constantcontact.com/product-blogs/social-media-marketing/what-the-heck-is-pinterest-and-why-should-you-care/ (Constant Contact, February 16, 2012)
[168] Ibid.
[169] Ryan Pinkham "10 Things You Need to Do When Getting Started on Pinterest" http://blogs.constantcontact.com/product-blogs/social-media-marketing/getting-started-on-pinterest/ (Constant Contact, August 9, 2012)
[170] Ibid.

171 Cynthia Sanchez "How to Repin on Pinterest Strategically" http://www.ohsopinteresting.com/how-to-repin-on-pinterest-strategically/ (OhsoPinteresting.com)
172 Jayson DeMers "6 Backstage Social Media Platforms Every Marketer Should Be Using" http://www.forbes.com/sites/jaysondemers/2014/08/26/6-backstage-social-media-platforms-every-marketer-should-be-using/ (*Forbes*, August 26, 2014)
173 A. Adam Glenn "How Educators Use Pinterest For Curation" http://blogs.kqed.org/mindshift/2012/03/how-educators-use-pinterest-for-curation/ (MindShift, March 21, 2012)
174 Om Malik "You Are What You Curate: Why Pinterest is Hot" https://gigaom.com/2012/01/04/you-are-what-you-curate-why-pinterest-is-hawt/ (Gigaom, January 4, 2012)
175 Greg Sterling "Report: 92 Percent of Pinterest Pins Made By Women" http://marketingland.com/report-92-percent-pinterest-pins-made-women-83394 (Marketing Land, May 12, 2014)
176 Marketing Charts Staff "User Demographic Highlights From 5 Major and Growing Social Networks" http://www.marketingcharts.com/online/user-demographic-highlights-from-5-major-and-growing-social networks-38939/ (Marketing Charts, January 6, 2014)
177 Matt McGee "Study: 70 Percent of Pinterest Users are There For Shopping Inspiration" http://marketingland.com/study-70-percent-pinterest-shopping-inspiration-24146 (Marketing Land, October 12, 2012)
178 Marketing Land Infographics http://marketingland.com/infographic-how-people-share-on-pinterest-63052 (Marketing Land, October 25, 2013)
179 Jeff Bullas "12 Awesome Social Media Facts and Statistics" http://www.jeffbullas.com/2013/09/20/12-awesome-social-media-facts-and-statistics-for-2013/ (Jeff Bullas Blog, ?)
180 Shea Bennett "This Week on Twitter: Social Media Stats 2014, Pinterest v Twitter v Facebook" http://www.mediabistro.com/allTwitter/top-10-Twitter-260114_b54492 (All Twitter, January 26, 2014)
181 White Glove Social Media "19 Mind Boggling Facts That Will Make you Join Pinterest Social Media Marketing" http://www.whiteglovesocialmedia.com/social-media-marketing-mind-boggling-facts-that-will-make-you-join-pinterest-social-media-marketing/ (White Glove Social Media, ?)
182 Shawn Hessinger "Pinterest Introduces Faster Location-Based Search" http://smallbiztrends.com/2014/06/new-pinterest-feature-faster-location-search.html (Small Business Trends, June 24, 2014)
183 Jessi Hempel "CEO Outlines the Future of Pinterest" http://fortune.com/2013/05/30/ceo-outlines-the-future-of-pinterest/ (*Fortune*, May 30, 2013)
184 http://digitalrelativity.com/pinterest-takeaways-from-brands-that-are-doing-it-right/
185 http://www.nytimes.com/2012/12/02/fashion/maria-popova-has-some-big-ideas.html?pagewanted=all&_r=0
186 http://www.nytimes.com/2012/12/02/fashion/maria-popova-has-some-big-ideas.html?pagewanted=all&_r=0
187 http://www.nytimes.com/2012/03/12/business/media/guidelines-proposed-for-content-aggregation-online.html?_r=0&adxnnl=1&pagewanted=all&adxnnlx=1406477257-oeMOHEnpqyMghrP9c6x7Gw
188 http://www.brainpickings.org/index.php/2012/03/09/Curators-code/
189 http://www.onthemedia.org/story/193718-Curators-code/
190 Molly Wood "A New Kind of Ecommerce Adds a Personal Touch: http://www.nytimes.com/2014/08/14/technology/personaltech/data-driven-shopping-with-the-personal-touch.html?_r=1 (*New York Times*, August 13, 2014)

191 https://www.birchbox.com/about/birchbox

192 https://www.birchbox.com/about/reward-points-terms

193 https://www.stitchfix.com/about

194 Molly Wood "A New Kind of Ecommerce Adds a Personal Touch" http://www.nytimes.com/2014/08/14/technology/personaltech/data-driven-shopping-with-the-personal-touch.html?_r=1 (*New York Times*, August 13, 2014)

195 Ibid.

196 Rachel King "Birch Box's CTO on the Beauty Secrets of Scaling a Global Startup" http://www.zdnet.com/q-and-a-birchboxs-cto-on-the-beauty-secrets-of-scaling-a-global-startup-7000022370/ (Between the Lines, November 1, 2013)

197 Yuliya Chernova "Birchbox Founders Stayed Disciplined, Refused to Be Boxed In" http://blogs.wsj.com/venturecapital/2014/05/05/birchbox-founders-stayed-disciplined-refused-to-be-boxed-in/ (*Wall Street Journal*, May 5, 2014)

198 Offerpop "3 Social Techniques Birchbox Uses to Reach the Well-Groomed Man" (Offerpop, February 20, 2013) http://www.offerpop.com/resources/blog/3-social-techniques-birchbox-uses-to-reach-the/

199 Dani Frankenhauser "Birchbox Explores the Beauty of 'Twitter Parties' http://contently.com/strategist/2012/05/14/birchbox-explores-the-beauty-of-Twitter-parties/ (Contently, May 14, 2012)

200 Sarah Halzack http://www.washingtonpost.com/news/business/wp/2014/08/19/online-shopping-is-the-future-so-why-do-so-many-Web-retailers-want-to-be-in-stores/ (*The Washington Post*, August 19, 2014)

201 Ibid.

202 Ibid.

203 Lexi Novak "We Tried It! Birch box Opens Its First Store in New York City" http://www.allure.com/beauty-trends/blogs/daily-beauty-reporter/2014/08/birchbox-opens-first-new-york-store.html (Daily Beauty Reporter, August 19, 2014)

204 Teresa Novellino "That New Birchbox Store Isn't Really About Selling Products" http://www.bizjournals.com/bizwomen/news/latest-news/2014/07/that-new-birchbox-store-isnt-really-about-selling.html (*The Business Journals*, July 23, 2014)

205 Ibid.

206 Tammy Tierney http://www.bizjournals.com/bizjournals/how-to/marketing/2014/08/how-to-build-your-own-subscription-box-business.html (The Business Journals, August 19, 2014)

207 Ibid.

208 Meghan Casserly "Birchbox Goes Global, Acquires Paris-Based Copycat 'JolieBox' http://www.forbes.com/sites/meghancasserly/2012/09/13/birchbox-goes-global-acquires-paris-based-copycat-joliebox/ (*Forbes*, September 13, 2012)

209 Interview with the author, 9/1/14

210 http://www.rohitbhargava.com/2009/09/manifesto-for-the-content-Curator-the-next-big-social-media-job-of-the-future.html

211 http://www.rohitbhargava.com/2011/03/the-5-models-of-content-curation.html

212 https://www.youtube.com/yt/press/statistics.html

213 http://www.forbes.com/sites/stevenrosenbaum/2012/10/11/youtubes-curation-vision-the-impact/

214 http://archive.wired.com/wired/archive/12.10/tail.html

215 "About Us" http://www.scoop.it/aboutus. Retrieved on 29 July 2014.

216 Leanna Johnson, "Why Scoop.It Is Becoming An Indispensible Learning Tool," http://www.teachthought.com/technology/why-scoopit-is-becoming-an-indispensable-learning-tool/. 18 Feb. 2013. Retrieved 29 July 2014.

[217] Rebecca Grant, "Scoop.it raises $2.6M to make everyone a publisher." http://venturebeat.com/2013/07/30/scoop-it-raises-2-6m-to-turn-anyone-into-a-publisher/. 30 June 2013. Retrieved 29 July 2014.

[218] K3Hamilton, "A Cultural History of Advertising," http://www.scoop.it/t/a-cultural-history-of-advertising. Retrieved 29 July 2014.

[219] The Law Offices of Bornstein & Bornstein and Bay Property Group, "Sharing Updates & Insights," http://www.scoop.it/t/bornstein-baypropertygroup. Retrieved 8 August 2014.

[220] Doug Peterson, "Groundhog Day" A collection of resources for Groundhog Day," http://www.scoop.it/t/groundhog-day. Retrieved 8 August 2014

[221] Doug Peterson, "QR-Codes: Resources that I've found useful for creating/using QR-Codes in Education," http://www.scoop.it/t/dp-qr-codes. Retrieved on 8 August 2014

[222] "Company Overview" http://www.crunchbase.com/organization/goojet. Retrieved 29 July 2014

[223] "Curata is a Web-based content marketing and content curation solution that helps you easily update your microsites in 20 minutes or less per day with new, fresh and remarkable content." http://www.one4marketing.nl/curata-0/. Retrieved 29 July 2014.

[224] "Curata, Inc. Description" http://launchpoint.marketo.com/curata-inc/884-curata-content-curation-software/. Retrieved 29 July 2014

[225] Christine Whittmore, "Content Talks Business Blog: Meet Pawan Deshpande, Content Curator and Curata CEO," http://simplemarketingnow.com/content-talks-business-blog/bid/126781/Meet-Pawan-Deshpande-Content-Curator-and-Curata-CEO. 23 May 2012. Retrieved 29 July 2014.

[226] Jessie Zubatkin, "Real World Examples of Content Curation Inspiration," http://bostinno.streetwise.co/channels/real-world-examples-of-content-curation-inspiration/. 30 Jan. 2013. Retrieved 29 July 2014.

[227] "Oregon Wine Newsroom," http://newsroom.oregonwine.org/. Retrieved 8 August 2014

[228] Pawan Deshpande, "4 Content Curation Tips You Can Take from Brand Success Stories," http://contentmarketinginstitute.com/2013/02/content-curation-tips-from-brand-success-stories/. 27 February 2013. Retrieved 8 August 2014

[229] "News & Press" "MITX awards Curata's Content Marketing Software as the Most Innovative B2B Technology in 2014," http://www.curata.com/press/press-release/?article=1045. 24 June 2014. Retrieved 29 July 2014.

[230] "About Us," http://list.ly/about. Retrieved 30 July 2014

[231] Mike Allton, "How List.ly Can Blow Up Blog Traffic," http://www.socialmediatoday.com/content/how-listly-can-blow-blog-traffic. 20 March 2013. Retrieved 30 July 2014

[232] Marie Ennis-O'Connor, "Patient Support Communities on Twitter," http://list.ly/list/4Uw-patient-support-communities-on-Twitter. Retrieved 30 July 2014.

[233] Doug Kessler, "Content Marketing Tools," http://list.ly/list/8KM-content-marketing-tools. Retrieved 8 August 2014

[234] Scott Scanlon, "Best History Books," http://list.ly/list/2Sn-best-history-books. Retrieved 8 August 2014.

[235] "Customer Profile: Storify Success," http://www.joyent.com/content/08-company/05-customers/14-storify/casestudy-storify.pdf. Retrieved 30 July 2014

[236] Mike Cassidy, "What Facebook $38 IPO means to the rest of us," https://storify.com/mikecassidy/we-have-a-facebook-stock-price-oh-my-god-oh-my-god. 7 August 2012. Retrieved 30 July 2014

[237] The White House Storify Page, "What #40dollars Means to Americans," https://storify.com/whitehouse/what-does-40dollars-mean-to-you. Retrieved on 8 August 2014.

[238] The United Nations Storify Page, "#67minutes of service," https://storify.com/un/mandela-day-67minutes. Retrieved 8 August 2014.

239 Alex Gamela, "BUNDLR IS A NEW CURATION TOOL AND CAN IT BE BETTER THAN STORIFY?," http://www.alexgamela.com/blog/2011/02/01/bundlr-is-a-new-curation-tool-and-can-it-be-better-than-storify/. 1 Feb. 2011. Retrieved 30 July 2014.

240 Alexandre Gamela, "Curation tool Bundlr sets to 'untangle the wed,'" http://blogs.journalism.co.uk/2011/02/01/new-curation-tool-bundlr-sets-sights-on-untangling-the-Web/. 1 Feb. 2011. Retrieved 30 July 2014

241 Alexandre Gamela, "Curation tool Bundlr sets to 'untangle the wed,'" http://blogs.journalism.co.uk/2011/02/01/new-curation-tool-bundlr-sets-sights-on-untangling-the-Web/. 1 Feb. 2011. Retrieved 30 July 2014

242 http://bundlr.com/b/news-rewired. Retrieved 30 July 2014

243 "Bundlr or iPhone on Vimeo," https://vimeo.com/76890542. December 2013. Retrieved 30 July 2014.

244 Anna Paczynska, "All Kinds of Wow," http://bundlr.com/b/all-kinds-of-wow. Retrieved 8 August 2014.

245 Anna Paczynska, "Shoes" http://bundlr.com/b/shoes14. Retrieved 8 August 2014.

246 Anna Paczynska, "furniture," http://bundlr.com/b/furni. Retrieved 8 August 2014.

247 Alexandre Gamela, "Curation tool Bundlr sets to 'untangle the wed,'" http://blogs.journalism.co.uk/2011/02/01/new-curation-tool-bundlr-sets-sights-on-untangling-the-Web/. 1 Feb. 2011. Retrieved 30 July 2014

248 http://www.curata.com/blog/copyright-images-how-to-avoid-and-curate-safely/

249 http://www.contentcurationmarketing.com/content-curation-copyright-ethics-fair-use/

250 http://www.contentcurationmarketing.com/content-curation-copyright-ethics-fair-use/

251 http://www.nytimes.com/2012/07/22/magazine/pinterest-tumblr-and-the-trouble-with-curation.html?pagewanted=all&_r=0

252 http://emergencyjournalism.net/curation-platforms/

253 http://allthingsd.com/20130227/cluster-app-aims-at-better-photo-curation-especially-for-the-lazy/

254 http://www.convinceandconvert.com/social-media-measurement/new-research-finds-the-curation-vs-creation-sweet-spot/

255 http://www.convinceandconvert.com/social-media-measurement/new-research-finds-the-curation-vs-creation-sweet-spot/

256 http://www.convinceandconvert.com/social-media-measurement/new-research-finds-the-curation-vs-creation-sweet-spot/

257 http://www.convinceandconvert.com/social-media-measurement/new-research-finds-the-curation-vs-creation-sweet-spot/

258 "Content Curation" WhatIs.com, http://whatis.techtarget.com/definition/content-curation (August, 2012)

259 http://www.masternewmedia.org/curation-for-education-and-learning/

260 Robin Good, "Why Curation Will Transform Education and Learning: 10 Key Reasons" http://www.masternewmedia.org/curation-for-education-and-learning/ (August 9, 2012)

261 Ibid.

262 Ibid.

263 Ibid.

264 Ibid.

265 Nancy White, "Curation in the Classroom" http://d2oinnovation.d2oblogs.org/2012/07/07/understanding-content-curation/ (July 7, 2012)

266 Ibid.

267 Ibid.

268 Ibid.

269 "Why Curation Soft" http://curationsoft.com/why-curationsoft/

270 Ibid.
271 https://www.diigo.com/about
272 Ibid.
273 Maggie, "Diigo Welcomes its 7th Million User with a Major Redesign" http://blog.diigo.com/2013/08/19/diigo-welcomes-its-7th-million-user-with-a-major-redesign/ (Diigo Blog, August 19, 2013)
274 "Dipity" http://teachinghistory.org/digital-classroom/tech-for-teachers/24620
275 Ed Young, "A Timeline of the Fukushima Disaster" (*Discover Magazine*, April 6, 2011) http://blogs.discovermagazine.com/notrocketscience/2011/04/06/a-timeline-of-the-fukushima-disaster/#.U-USj1Z9lgM
276 "Dipity" http://teachinghistory.org/digital-classroom/tech-for-teachers/24620
277 www.dipity.com
278 "Timelines: Dipity" http://www.digitize-me-captain.com/timelines-dipity/ (Digitize Me, Captain, Sept. 8, 2012)
279 http://www.alexa.com/siteinfo/dipity.com
280 https://evernote.com
281 Ibid.
282 http://elearningtags.com/elearning
283 Karla Gutierrez, "18 Mind-Blowing eLearning Statistics You Need to Know" http://info.shiftelearning.com/blog/bid/247473/18-Mind-Blowing-eLearning-Statistics-You-Need-To-Know (Shift's eLearning Blog, November 29, 2012)
284 Ibid.
285 Christopher Pappas, "List of eLearning Twitter Hashtags" http://elearningindustry.com/list-of-elearning-Twitter-hashtags-being-used-right-now (eLearning Basics, October 31, 2012)
286 Karla Gutierrez, "18 Mind-Blowing eLearning Statistics You Need to Know" http://info.shiftelearning.com/blog/bid/247473/18-Mind-Blowing-eLearning-Statistics-You-Need-To-Know (Shift's eLearning Blog, November 29, 2012)
287 http://en.support.symbaloo.com/knowledgebase/articles/224511-what-is-symbaloo
288 Francys Vallecillo, "Jury is Out: Ecommerce vs Brick-and-Mortar" http://www.worldpropertychannel.com/north-america-commercial-news/ecommerce-trends-ecommerce-sales-data-retail-shopping-declines-shopping-mall-trends-john-ellis-randy-anderson-cbre-research-amazon-consumer-shopping-report-7977.php, 7 Feb/. 2014. Retrieved 4 August 2014
289 Francys Vallecillo, "Jury is Out: Ecommerce vs Brick-and-Mortar" http://www.worldpropertychannel.com/north-america-commercial-news/ecommerce-trends-ecommerce-sales-data-retail-shopping-declines-shopping-mall-trends-john-ellis-randy-anderson-cbre-research-amazon-consumer-shopping-report-7977.php, 7 Feb/. 2014. Retrieved 4 August 2014
290 Carley Botelho, "The Pros and Cons of Online Retailers vs. Brick-and-Mortar" http://www.business2community.com/strategy/pros-cons-online-retailers-vs-brick-mortar-stores-0848992#!bynLDx, 22 April 2014. Retrieved 5 August 2014
291 Francys Vallecillo, "Jury is Out: Ecommerce vs Brick-and-Mortar" http://www.worldpropertychannel.com/north-america-commercial-news/ecommerce-trends-ecommerce-sales-data-retail-shopping-declines-shopping-mall-trends-john-ellis-randy-anderson-cbre-research-amazon-consumer-shopping-report-7977.php, 7 Feb/. 2014. Retrieved 4 August 2014
292 Lydia Dishman, "Glance is Zappos Gamble on Curated Ecommerce" http://www.fastcompany.com/3006108/buyology/glance-zapposs-gamble-curated-ecommerce, 21 Feb. 2013. Retrieved on 5 August 2014

293 Lydia Dishman, "Glance is Zappos Gamble on Curated Ecommerce" http://www.fastcompany.com/3006108/buyology/glance-zapposs-gamble-curated-ecommerce, 21 Feb. 2013. Retrieved on 5 August 2014
294 Lydia Dishman, "Glance is Zappos Gamble on Curated Ecommerce" http://www.fastcompany.com/3006108/buyology/glance-zapposs-gamble-curated-ecommerce, 21 Feb. 2013. Retrieved on 5 August 2014
295 Kevin Smith, "Take a Look at 'The Fancy' App Made by the Company Apple Is Interested In Buying" http://www.businessinsider.com/the-fancy-app-guide-2012-8?op=1#ixzz39l6vy833, 12 August 2012. Retrieved 5 August 2014
296 Cedar Pasori, "Interview: Joseph Einhorn, Founder of The Fancy" http://www.complex.com/style/2012/05/interview-joseph-einhorn-founder-of-the-fancy, 7 May 2012. Retrieved 5 August 2014.
297 http://en.wikipedia.org/wiki/Fancy_(social_network_service)
298 Kevin Smith, "Take a Look at 'The Fancy' App Made by the Company Apple Is Interested In Buying" http://www.businessinsider.com/the-fancy-app-guide-2012-8?op=1#ixzz39l6vy833, 12 August 2012. Retrieved 5 August 2014
299 Felicia C. Sullivan, "Interview: Shauna Mei, CEO/Founder of AHAlife" http://www.huffingtonpost.com/felicia-c-sullivan/interview-shauna-mei-ceof_b_773812.html, 29 Oct. 2014. Retrieved 7 August 2014
300 Leena Rao, "AHAlife Raises $10.1M to Curate and Sell Hard-to-Find, Luxury Items From Around the World" http://techcrunch.com/2012/04/26/ahalife-raises-10-1m-to-curate-and-sell-hard-to-find-luxury-products-from-around-the-world/, 26 April 2012. Retrieved 4 August 2014
301 "About Us" http://www.ahalife.com/about. Retrieved 4 August 2014
302 Leena Rao, "AHAlife Raises $10.1M to Curate and Sell Hard-to-Find, Luxury Items From Around the World" http://techcrunch.com/2012/04/26/ahalife-raises-10-1m-to-curate-and-sell-hard-to-find-luxury-products-from-around-the-world/, 26 April 2012. Retrieved 5 August 2014
303 Erin Griffith, "Why Would AHAlife, a luxury commerce site buy Kaptur, a photo-sharing app?" http://pando.com/2013/07/24/why-would-ahalife-a-luxury-commerce-site-buy-a-kaptur-photo-sharing-app/, 24 July 2013. Retrieved 4 August 2014
304 Jessi Hempel "How Ben Lerer Competes with Amazon" http://fortune.com/2014/02/24/how-ben-lerer-competes-with-amazon, 24 Feb. 2014. Retrieved 7 August 2014
305 Claire Cain Miller, "At Thrillist, Mingling Commerce and Content" 20 March 2011. Retrieved 7 August 2014
306 "America's Most Promising Companies List" http://www.forbes.com/most-promising-companies/list/. Retrieved 7 August 2014
307 http://www.thrillist.com/about
308 "About Us" http://www.thrillist.com/about. Retrieved 7 August 2014
309 Jessi Hempel "How Ben Lerer Competes with Amazon" http://fortune.com/2014/02/24/how-ben-lerer-competes-with-amazon, 24 Feb. 2014. Retrieved 7 August 2014
310 "Events" http://events.thrillist.com/bestdayofyourlife. Retrieved 7 August 2014
311 "FAQ" http://www.shoedazzle.com/faq.htm. Retrieved 7 August 2014
312 "FAQ" http://www.shoedazzle.com/faq.htm. Retrieved 7 August 2014
313 iTunes. https://itunes.apple.com/us/app/kim-kardashian-hollywood/id860822992?mt=8. Retrieved 7 August 2014
314 Maseen Zeigler "Why 'Kim Kardashian: Hollywood' is a $200 Million Hit App" https://itunes.apple.com/us/app/kim-kardashian-hollywood/id860822992?mt=8. 16 July 2014. Retrieved 7 August 2014

[315] WWD Staff, "Truly Fast Fashion: H&M Lagerfeld Line Sells Out in Hours" http://www.wwd.com/fashion-news/fashion-features/truly-fast-fashion-h-m-8217-s-lagerfeld-line-sells-out-in-hours-593089?full=true. 15 Nov. 2004. Retrieved 7 August 2014.

[316] "Here It Is Versace for H &M the Complete Collection" http://fashionista.com/2011/10/here-it-is-versace-for-hm-collection-the-complete-collection#versacehm86_v_18oct11_pr_b_320x480. Retrieve 7 August 2014

[317] Harrods Girl, "I Am Fashion: Stella McCartney" http://iamfashion.blogspot.se/2005/11/stella-mccartney-for-hm.html. 11 November 2005. Retrieved on 5 August 2014

[318] "Our History" http://about.hm.com/en/About/facts-about-hm/people-and-history/history.html. Retrieved on 5 August 2014

[319] "Target Unveils New Design Partnership Program" http://pressroom.target.com/news/target-unveils-new-design-partnership-221743, 13 Jan. 2013. Retrieved 7 August 2014

[320] "About Us" http://www.curateboutique.com/about-us/. Retrieved 7 August 2014

[321] Rea McNamara, "Fashion as Art: 5 game-changing fashion Curators you need to know" http://www.fashionmagazine.com/society/2014/02/04/5-fashion-Curators-you-need-to-know/. 4 Feb. 2014. Retrieved 6 August 2014

[322] Rayi, "Nights at the Museum with Olivier Saillard" http://rayipress.com/nights-at-the-museum-with-olivier-saillard/. 6 July 2014. Retrieved 7 August 2014

[323] Kimberly Lyn, "Interview: Elizabeth Semmelhack, Senior Curator of the Bata Shoe Museum" http://www.thesoulsofmyshoes.com/2013/11/25/interview-elizabeth-semmelhack-senior-Curator-of-the-bata-shoe-museum/. 25 Nov. 2013. Retrieved 6 August 2014

[324] Philippe Pourhashemi "MoMu director Kaat Debo on its first decade" http://thewordmagazine.com/style/momu-director-kaat-debo-on-the-museums-first-decade-buying-the-right-pieces-and-the-challenges-of-conservation/. 14 Nov. 2012. Retrieved 6 August 2014

[325] Julia Petrov, "Cross-purposes: museum display and material culture" http://www.freepatentsonline.com/article/Cross-Currents/296699246.html, 1 June 2012. Retrieved 6 August 2014

[326] Carrie Whitehead, "Zappos Labs: The Frontier of Online Retail is Curation" http://www.psfk.com/2013/04/online-retail-curation.html#!byroTi. 28 April 2013. Retrieved 5 August 2014

[327] http://www.huffingtonpost.com/rachel-schwartzmann/looklab-a-pioneer-of-inte_b_1408714.html

[328] Nadia Buick & Madeleine King, "Curating Fashion Online" http://designonline.org.au/content/curating-fashion-online/. Retrieved 5 August 2014

[329] http://www.slideshare.net/corinnew/building-thought-leadership-through-content-curation

[330] http://books.google.com/books?id=fdTQZZo-4U4C&lpg=PA50&ots=p3XtG_86SA&dq=Content%20curation%20can%20take%20many%20forms%3A%20feeds%2C%20channels%2C%20it%20can%20appear%20on%20blogs&pg=PA49#v=onepage&q&f=false

[331] http://www.toprankblog.com/2010/06/content-marketing-curation-context/

[332] http://www.forbes.com/sites/ciocentral/2012/06/04/4-reasons-why-content-curation-has-gone-mainstream/

[333] https://contentequalsmoney.com/can-proper-content-curation-feed-your-thought-leadership/

[334] http://www.toprankblog.com/2010/06/content-marketing-curation-context/

[335] https://za.news.yahoo.com/content-curation-101-benefits-business-5-very-useful-050019535.html

[336] http://www.contentstrategyhub.com/content-curation-guide/

[337] www.huffingtonpost.com/tag/**curation**-nation/

[338] http://www.shelaunched.com

[339] http://theentrepreneurwithin.org/about/founder/

[340] http://www.ted.com/speakers/chris_anderson_ted

[341] http://stlCurator.com/team/

[342] http://www.venturehacks.com

[343] http://www.amazon.com/Permission-Marketing-Turning-Strangers-Customers/dp/0684856360

[344] http://gigaom.com/2012/03/13/its-not-curation-or-aggregation-its-just-how-the-Internet-works/

[345] http://www.forbes.com/sites/avaseave/2014/01/29/unlocking-curation-data-drives-content-first-community/

345http://www.forbes.com/sites/avaseave/2014/01/29/unlocking-curation-data-drives-content-first-community/

15747081R00204

Made in the USA
Middletown, DE
19 November 2014